TRAVEL

The Grand Palace, Bangkok.

TRAVEL

Sue Seddon

Foreword by JOHN JULIUS NORWICH

Published by
ALAN SUTTON PUBLISHING and THOMAS COOK
to celebrate 150 years of travel

First published in 1991 by

ALAN SUTTON PUBLISHING LTD · PHOENIX MILL · STROUD · GLOUCESTERSHIRE · UK

ALAN SUTTON PUBLISHING INC · WOLFEBORO FALLS · NH 03896–0848 · USA

and

THOMAS COOK PUBLISHING · THORPE WOOD · PETERBOROUGH · UK

British Library Cataloguing in Publication Data

Seddon, Sue
  Travel.
  1. Travel. History
  I. Title
  910.4

  ISBN 0-86299-903-0

Library of Congress Cataloging in Publication Data
Seddon, Sue.
  Travel / Sue Seddon.
    p.   cm.
  Includes bibliographical references.
  ISBN 0-86299-903-0
  1. Travel–History.   I. Title.
  G151.S43   1991
  910.4–dc20   91–4123
                                      CIP

Typeset in 10/13 Baskerville.
Typesetting and origination by
Alan Sutton Publishing Limited.
Colour separation by
Yeo Valley Reprographics Ltd.
Printed in Great Britain by
Eagle Colourbooks Ltd, Glasgow.

Contents

LIGNES AERIENNES
G. LATÉCOÈRE
TOULOUSE
Perpignan
Barcelone
France
Espagne
Maroc
Valence
Alicante
Malaga
Gibraltar
Tanger
Ceuta
Larache
Oran
Alger
Rabat
Casablanca

Foreword

In 1937 I made my first journey to what used to
be called 'The Continent'. I remember it as if it
were yesterday: the sandwiches on the boat-train
as we rattled through Kentish orchards; the smell
of the *Maid of Orleans* as she butted her way out of
Dover harbour into a distinctly choppy sea and, an
hour later, that of the garlicky blue-smocked
porters who came on board at Calais; the huge
and hedgeless fields of Normandy; the excitement
of the taxi-ride from the Gare du Nord and the
view of the Eiffel Tower from the hotel window.
All that day my seven-year-old heart seemed to
beat at twice its normal rate; and to the rhythm of
the train, the same words kept drumming through
my mind: 'I'm *abroad*!'

Fifty-six years later, stepping off a ship or an
aeroplane, I still experience a faint echo of that
same thrill; and many readers of the pages that
follow will, I fervently hope, do the same. But by
now – for most of us at any rate – foreign travel
has become an integral part of our existence. Even
if it plays no part in our professional work, we
probably have at least one annual holiday abroad
to look forward to; and whether that holiday is
based on sun, sea or snow, on art, archaeology or
music, or on the exploration and enjoyment of the
wild blue yonder, we nowadays tend to think of it
as more of a birthright than a privilege, something
without which our lives would be sadly – perhaps
almost unfairly – diminished.

Is there any other subject towards which, in half
a century, our attitudes have changed so
dramatically? Thomas Cook, the co-publishers of
this volume, it is true, can look back on a history
three times as long as that; yet even in pre-war
years they were catering for a tiny minority of the
population. My own father seldom voluntarily
went beyond France and Italy; my grandfather, so
far as I know, never crossed the Channel in his

life. The truth is, however, that the very idea of
travelling for pleasure is relatively recent. To men
of the Middle Ages it would have seemed absurd:
for them, virtually the only reasons for leaving
home were trade, pilgrimage and war. In the
sixteenth century the new art of diplomacy added
another. But it was only at the beginning of the
eighteenth, with the increasing popularity of the
Grand Tour, that travel became desirable for its
own sake; and only a hundred years after that,
with the end of the Napoleonic Wars, that the
fashion spread outside the aristocracy.

Now, thanks largely to Thomas Cook (to whom
all congratulations on their 150th anniversary),
more people than ever before can – and do – look
upon the world as their oyster. It is entirely right
and proper that they should; at the same time this
state of affairs brings its own dangers. No
intelligent traveller of today can fail to see how
quickly uncontrolled tourism can destroy the
world's heritage, both natural and cultural, or to
recognize that there must be limits to the quantity
of visitors that a given building, or even a given
city, can accept in the course of a year; nor can
any of us get any real pleasure out of wandering
round St Mark's Square or the Sistine Chapel, the
Acropolis or the Taj Mahal in a crowd normally
encountered only in Selfridge's three shopping
days before Christmas. And so, I believe, our
attitude to travel will soon be changing again.

Briefly, we shall no longer take the great
honeypot sites of the world for granted. Very soon
(pray God before it is too late) we shall find the
authorities responsible for their preservation
imposing quotas – if not on individual travellers,
then at least on groups – and we shall grow
accustomed to having to book our tour to Venice
or Rome, Athens or Agra, two or even three years
ahead. This may seem a retrograde step, but in
fact there will be no cause for complaint: what
does it really matter, after all, if we have to wait a
little – so long as we can then see these great
monuments as they deserve to be seen, and
without contributing, by sheer force of numbers,
to their destruction? Meanwhile we can look
forward to holidays every bit as enjoyable –
perhaps even more so – concentrating for a change
on rather lesser-known sites, which we shall have
far more space and leisure to appreciate and
which, incidentally, we may well find that we
prefer. For the world is full of wonders: more than
enough for all of us. And does not half the fun of
travel lie in the excitement of discovery?

John Julius Norwich

CHAPTER *1*

'Here be Dragons'

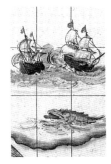

AS DAY DAWNED in the remote jungle of the Venezuelan Amazonas the traveller reached for his sodden clothes and rotting boots, shook them free of invading ants and poisonous hairy caterpillars, and crawled from his smelly, fungus-covered mosquito net. Not for the first time on a trip, the naturalist, writer and traveller Redmond O'Hanlon fantasized about waking between crisp, dry sheets. Even adventurous travellers like O'Hanlon crave home comforts, so why do people travel?

Opposite The towering canopy of South American rainforest stretches to the horizon.

Early map-makers sprinkled the oceans of the world with spouting sea monsters to denote the unknown terrors of the deep and the dangers of uncharted waters.

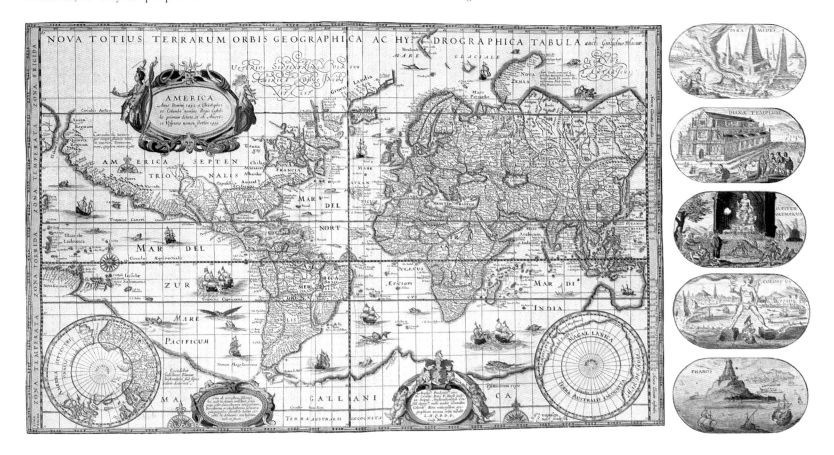

The reasons are numerous and sometimes complex but curiosity about the planet on which we live is a prime motivator. People have always travelled to see the world and to find out how other people live. For centuries the outer edges of the world map dwindled to empty lands and seas where early cartographers filled the vast spaces with sea monsters and mythical creatures which gave rise to the figure of speech 'Here be Dragons'. Circumnavigators, explorers, soldiers, sailors, merchants and government officials of past

Chaucer's pilgrims travelled only a short distance from London to Canterbury, but to embark on a pilgrimage was one of the ways in which an ordinary citizen of the Middle Ages could travel abroad.

centuries travelled to draw the map of the world that we know today. There are few places on the globe unmapped, but there are millions of people in the world who have never seen the sea, or mountains, or a desert, or a snow-covered landscape, and many of them want to experience such places because the unknown is one of the great pleasures of travel.

Travellers may be inquisitive about the world, but they also travel to make discoveries about themselves. The mythical beasts on the edges of the map have been dispelled, but they have been replaced by the personal dragon of self knowledge; how will the traveller deal with the test of physical and mental endurance and face the challenge of adventure and danger? Crossing a busy road is the biggest risk that most of us take in our daily lives, travel gives the opportunity to see how we cope with the unknown. It can, but does not necessarily, mean paddling down the Orinoco alone, with a two week ration of half a ship's biscuit and some rancid coconut milk. Until you've tried, just using the phone or getting bread and baked beans in a language you cannot speak, can be quite a challenge.

People who travel are as varied as their journeys. They range from the lone back-packer who stuffs a volume of Descartes into the pocket

One for the album. A camel poses for a tourist to Egypt in the 1950s.

Opposite Past and present meet in Hong Kong harbour today.

of her shorts and forgets to take spare socks, to
the package holiday-maker who packs a change of
silk shirt for every evening he is going to be away.
There is, of course, a difference between the
tourist and the traveller. The *Shorter Oxford
Dictionary* defines a tourist as 'one who travels for
pleasure or culture, visiting a number of places',
but a traveller can do that. These days the word
'tourist' is generally associated with the package
holiday-maker who follows a known itinerary and
for whom all the arrangements are made by a
travel company. For some people, the joy of being
a tourist is that they don't have to think,
everything is done for them.

The traveller on the other hand is a free spirit.
He or she may choose to travel with friends, but
the true traveller sets out to make an independent,
unhurried journey to the unknown, without
supervision, avoiding tourist shrines and travelling
where few foreign feet tread. But whether traveller
or tourist, both travel, or 'make a journey of some
length to distant countries' as given in one strict
dictionary definition.

There are plenty of ordinary reasons for
travelling: business; visits to family or friends; for
culture or history; sea, sun and sand; religion or
health; education; shopping; food and wines; or
just plain fun. But which of us, locked behind a
desk or in a queue at the supermarket check-out,
has not had an overwhelming desire to drop
everything, run into the street, hail a passing cab
and make for the nearest airport to catch a plane
to anywhere? The frustration of modern life can be
so great that the destination scarcely matters.

Travel can be an escape from the routine
drudgery of life, from duties and obligations, or a
broken heart, parents, the law, or the tax man.
Escape can be a strong motivation for travel, but
according to the great traveller Freya Stark, 'The
true wanderer, whose travels are happiness, goes
out not to shun, but to seek.' If escape seems a
negative reason to go on a journey, travel can
transform it into a positive one. Travel changes
perspectives, it gives the traveller a new set of
horizons and a chance to even up the sense of
proportion with which he or she views life. All this
can manifest itself in the simple relief of getting
back to civilization, supermarket queues and all.

Why do some travellers make life so difficult for
themselves? They pick the remotest jungles, the
most primitive trains, the roughest country to
cycle through. Seneca, the Roman author and
politician, claimed that men travel '. . . because
they are tired of soft living and always seek after
something which eludes them'. Most travellers will
explain, like the writer and traveller Paul
Theroux, that unless the journey has been difficult
they do not feel as if they have been travelling. On
this point they have much in common with

The Himalayas, one of the world's most sought-after destinations,
draw both tourists and travellers to Nepal to experience their
enigmatic beauty.

travellers from the past: the word 'travel' comes from 'travail' and until the second half of the nineteenth century travel was such hard and dangerous work that few people contemplated it. If they did set out on a journey, it was usually on business or a pilgrimage or to go to war.

It could take fourteen weeks to complete the

Robert Louis Stevenson (*seated centre back row*) at Vailima on the island of Upolu. After a lifetime of travelling, the Scottish novelist finally settled in Western Samoa in 1890, four years before his death.

gruelling journey on foot from London to Rome in the Middle Ages. Major routes were cart-tracks and marauding bandits and unscrupulous innkeepers thought nothing of robbery and murder. When Celia Fiennes travelled round England and Scotland on horseback in the late seventeenth century, it was a courageous and unconventional thing for a twenty-year-old woman to do. There were few signposts and the rough roads had waterfilled potholes deep enough to drown a man – if the footpads didn't get him first. Travel for pleasure was almost unheard of until the nineteenth century when Robert Louis Stevenson wrote, 'For my part, I travel not to go anywhere, but to go. I travel for travel's sake. The great affair is to move.' It was then that the pioneers of modern travel set in motion the age of travel in which we are so lucky to live.

Opposite Limestone cliffs and islands jut from the sea near Krabi, Thailand.

CHAPTER *2*

'The cloud-moving wind'

WALL AFTER WALL of raging water rose up and thundered on to the strange craft intent on destroying it and the frail humans clinging to it for their lives. Finally a sheer mountain of a wave smashed over the raft with a furious roar and swept it further on to the reef away from the pounding terror. The men on the raft unclamped their life-saving fingers from the balsa wood, uncurled their bodies braced against the fury of the Pacific, and waded through calm lagoon waters to the beach. 'I was completely overwhelmed' wrote Thor Heyerdahl later. 'I sank down on my knees and thrust my fingers into the dry warm sand.'

It was the successful end of the Kon-Tiki expedition. Heyerdahl, five companions and a sulky parrot had drifted 4,300 nautical miles across the Pacific Ocean on a balsa wood raft to prove Heyerdahl's theory that South American people could have travelled across the Pacific to become the ancestors of the Polynesian islanders. At first Kon-Tiki's journey appeared foolhardy, experts said that the raft would become waterlogged and sink like a stone, but the companions went ahead anyway. Braving storms and great creatures of the deep including the whale shark, they sailed hopefully for the most romantic of destinations, a coral island, and succeeded. They waded ashore on the Polynesian atoll of Raroia on 7 August 1947 just over three months after leaving Peru.

The world was captivated by the romance of the journey: six young travellers faced the dangers of the unknown and the elements with courage, tenacity and a debonair spirit of adventure. Ordinary mortals, chained to the pay packet, longed to have travelled on Kon-Tiki.

The still waters of a Polynesian island.

Opposite Kon-Tiki sails the Pacific. *Inset* Thor Heyerdahl at the steering rig.

Some travellers take up the challenge of lone journeys: a test of endurance in Arctic conditions. *Inset* Robyn Davidson crossed 1,700 miles of the formidable western desert of Australia with two camels and a dog for company.

As weather, work and the frenzy of city life threaten our sanity, the urge to flee from it all and to hell with the consequences, sweeps over the mind like a tsunami. For most people the tidal wave recedes after clinching a deal with the travel agent for a two week package holiday. But for some the undertow is too strong and they are

Milford Sound, New Zealand. Cook charted the coast of New Zealand on his first voyage of exploration, 1768–71. *Inset* Captain James Cook (1728–79). The remarkable navigator and cartographer circumnavigated the Antarctic but was killed in Hawaii on his third voyage.

sucked away to navigate unexplored tributaries of the Amazon, encounter the tribes of remotest Papua New Guinea, cross Australia by camel, or Asia by bicycle, or walk to the North Pole – alone. Matsuo Basho, a seventeenth-century Japanese poet and traveller, called the compulsion to travel 'the cloud-moving wind'. He wrote: 'The gods seem to have possessed my soul and turned it inside out . . . so that it was impossible for me to stay idle at home.'

It was (and is) impossible for many other travellers to stay at home too. Some travel to encounter different people and ways of life, others travel to reach a particular destination: the peak of an unconquered mountain, the far side of a desert or continent, the source of a river. Marco Polo travelled in the hope of trade with China; James Cook charted coasts and waters of New Zealand, Australia and the Pacific unknown to Europeans; achievement, adventure, glory and gain motivated explorers like the early circumnavigators and the seekers of the North West Passage.

Most travellers suffered appalling hardship and danger, none more so than the great Victorian explorers. In the year that Thomas Cook organized his first excursion from Leicester to Loughborough, David Livingstone first set foot in

SOUTH AFRICA

THREE ESCORTED TOURS

David Livingstone arrives at an African village. *Inset* Tourists now reach Victoria Falls: poster advertising its natural wonders.

Africa. Over the next twenty-eight years, driven by missionary zeal and the fire of exploration, Livingstone crossed the continent, followed the course of several vast African rivers including the Zambezi, and discovered Lake Malawi, Lake Ngami and the massive waterfall on the Zambezi which he named after Queen Victoria. His wife, Mary, accompanied him on his early forays, but in 1862, while travelling on the Zambezi, she caught a fever and died, worn out by the privations of travel and child bearing – her fifth child was born under a camel thorn bush on a trek through arid wastes of the interior; her fourth child, born on an earlier trek, had lived only six weeks.

Livingstone frequently seemed oblivious of his

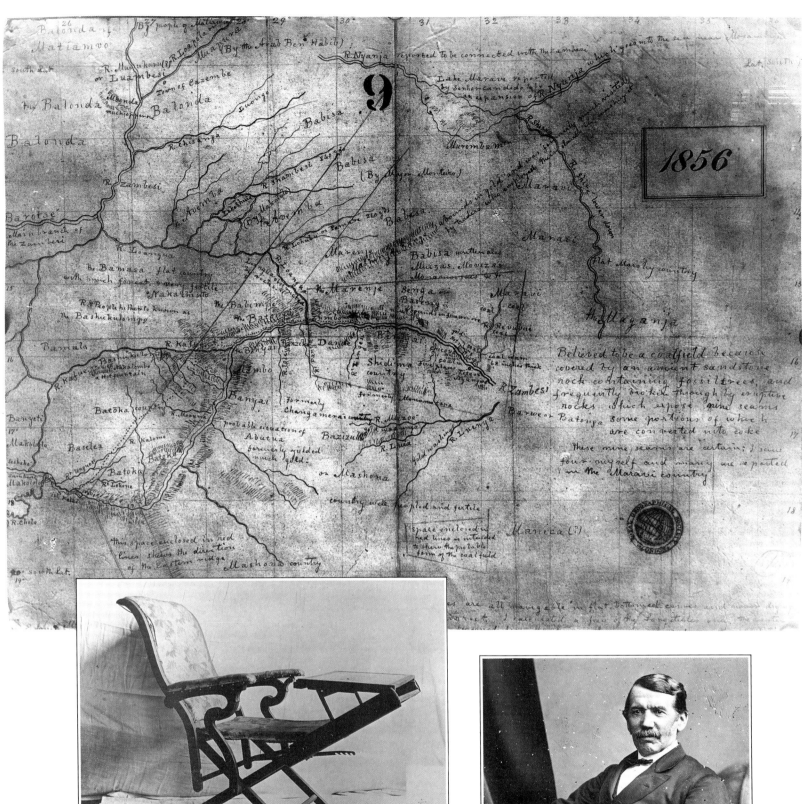

Top Livingstone's map of the Zambezi, 1856. *Above* The folding chair used by Livingstone on his expedition to Lake Nyasa (now Malawi). *Right* David Livingstone (1813–73), Scottish missionary and explorer. His body lies in Westminster Abbey, but his heart is buried in Africa.

Overleaf Victoria Falls named by Livingstone in 1855.

wife's sufferings, perhaps because he walked thousands of miles and endured fever, dysentery, near starvation, assaults by hostile tribes and was attacked by a lion. 'Growling horribly close to my ear, he shook me as a terrier dog does a rat,' he wrote. In 1866 Livingstone went to explore the watersheds of the Zambezi Congo (Zaire) and the Nile. By 1871 there was no word from him, he had disappeared into the interior of the great continent and the western world thought their hero dead. The *New York Herald* dispatched the journalist Henry Morton Stanley to find him, which he did on the famous encounter of 10 November 1871 at Ujiji, near Lake Tanganyika.

Sir Richard Burton, who described danger as the 'salt of pleasure', also travelled through central Africa. With John Hanning Speke he set out to discover the source of the Nile. Suffering fever, blindness and paralysis, they reached Lake Tanganyika in 1857 but it was Speke who eventually found Lake Victoria and realized that it was the reservoir which fed the great river.

Burton was an accomplished soldier, writer, and anthropologist, a brilliant linguist, swordsman and traveller. In 1853 he travelled to Mecca, which was such a dangerous trip for a European that he travelled as a Muslim pilgrim. So complete was his disguise that he was circumcised before the journey. In spite of the dangers, he mixed with Muslim pilgrims and performed all the religious rites, making copious notes of everything he saw. Burton travelled to observe and communicate, which made him different from most explorers of the day, but he too could be touched by the inexplicable fever of travel: '. . . some thousand miles up a river with an infinitesimal prospect of returning! I ask myself "Why?" and the only echo is "damned fool . . . the Devil drives."'

Men did not have a monopoly of travel, or of disguise. Alexandra David-Neel, the French traveller and explorer, travelled through Tibet in the 1920s. It was a rugged journey: the only known wheel in Tibet was the prayer wheel. In 1924 Madame Neel was the first European woman to enter Lhasa, the capital city of Tibet, and she had to travel disguised as an ignorant and grimy old country woman. It was so successful that she was beaten by the authorities for daring to walk where only the rich were permitted to stroll.

Mary Kingsley was also an intrepid traveller, but she stuck to the conventional dress of a Victorian lady, which on one occasion saved her life. Striding through Africa dressed in bonnet, high-necked blouse and long wool skirt, in search of beetles and fish to study, the ground beneath her gave way and she fell fifteen feet into an animal trap with twelve-inch long ebony spikes. 'It is at these times that you realize the blessings of a good thick skirt', she reported after her rescue.

Below Sir Richard Burton (1821–90). A traveller of extraordinary audacity, of whom Mitford wrote 'Burton had dared and done more almost than any man living'. *Bottom* Mary Kingsley (1862–1900). A brave, self-reliant and practical traveller whose sensible clothes saved her life.

'Had I paid heed to the advice of many people in England . . . and adopted masculine garments, I should have been spiked to the bone, and done for.'

Miss Kingsley was a practical woman; she had spent years housekeeping for her family and was thirty before she left on the first of her journeys to

The four stone figures of Rameses II at Abu Simbel today. In 1968 they were raised to their present position to escape inundation by the rising waters of a man-made lake.

West Africa in 1893, taking with her boots, blankets and a hot-water bottle. 'My mind', she said 'was set on going and I had to go.' Rudyard Kipling said of her: 'Being human, she must have been afraid of something, but one never found out what it was.'

In 1873, only two years after Stanley met Livingstone, Amelia B. Edwards was on a sketching holiday in France. The weather was appalling but instead of retreating to England, Amelia and her companion decided to go to Egypt. The result of her impetuosity was a thousand-mile journey up the Nile and a book about her adventures published in 1877. Like Mary Kingsley she was down-to-earth and when her expedition reached Abu Simbel she was horrified to see that the colossal figure of Rameses II was disfigured by plaster left on it fifty years before by an enthusiastic cast-maker. Her crew were idle so she armed them with brushes and mops and set them to scrub the magnificent monument clean. It took them three afternoons.

Amelia B. Edwards supervises the cleaning of one of the colossal statues of Rameses II at the entrance of the temple at Abu Simbel. The scaffolding, explains Miss Edwards in her book, was improvised from spars and oars.

Amelia may not have been in the same league as the great adventurers who scale mountain peaks, cross oceans and the icy wastes of the Antarctic and Arctic or shoot the white water rapids of unnavigable rivers, but she was a real traveller, ranked among those who actually get up and go, sacrificing security and facing the cold disdain of their bank managers. Theirs is the high romance of travel. The rest of us travel those kinds of journeys vicariously, slumped in a winter armchair reading accounts of Himalayan kingdoms reached only by months of walking, or of chucking in the job, mortgaging the house and sailing to the spice islands with oriental pirates.

In spite of the recent popularity of travel books, writing about travel is nothing new; the ancient Greeks and Romans wrote accounts of their journeys, as did medieval pilgrims and merchants. Réné Caillié, the first European to reach Timbuktu was inspired by reading *Robinson Crusoe*, a travel book of sorts. It took Caillié eleven years of meticulous planning and a further year to reach the fabled city in 1828, which turned out to be rather a disappointment to him after such a hazardous journey. In 1844 William Makepeace Thackeray managed to get P & O to give him a free passage on a voyage to Athens, Constantinople, Jerusalem and Cairo and earned money by writing about the trip afterwards. Mark Twain's *Innocents Abroad*, an account of his travels in Europe and the Near East, published in 1869, sold about 125,000 copies within the first three years of publication.

The travel writer is almost exclusively a twentieth-century phenomenon. Whether they are primarily travellers who write or writers who travel does not matter. Most have the compulsion to travel and then to write about it; their books may subsequently fund their next trip. Dervla Murphy, the Irish traveller, who has written several books about her travels with a bicycle across India and Asia, travels purely to enjoy herself, and her books about her adventures give enjoyment and inspiration to armchair travellers.

Colin Thubron, traveller and award-winning travel writer, was influenced by Freya Stark's style: 'I was absolutely fascinated by the way she could make certain words shine.' Dame Freya Stark, one of the greatest travellers, is an inspiration in herself. She began travelling in earnest in 1927 when she was thirty-four; later she crossed Persia, her long hair flowing, because she felt marginally safer from attack if bandits could see that she was a woman. Not that she was afraid; she once said that she travelled to seek out danger to 'silence fear' so that she could reach the end of her days 'free from that mortal weakness'. She tackled the Himalayas at eighty-eight, occasionally allowing porters to carry her pick-a-back across impossible terrain.

The All Nations and Mary Magdalene Churches in Jerusalem.

Mark Twain (1835–1910), author of one of the first popular travel books, in his car, 1907.

However well charted the world may be there is still adventure, danger and hardship for some travellers to endure: Christina Dodwell experienced 'cold terror' while crossing the rapids of the Laigap River in Papua New Guinea; Dervla Murphy survived an attack by wolves and several rape attempts; Rosie Atkins, travelling round the

Freya Stark in the garden of her house in Italy. 'You can be a traveller in your own garden', she said. 'When everybody travels it will make it awfully pleasant to sit at home.' *Left* The Himalayas provide a magnificent backdrop to this Buddhist temple in Ladakh.

world with her husband and two children, was trapped overnight in a battered old coach by a landslide in Ladakh. As the wheels skidded on the edge of the precipice a storm tried to hurl the coach and her family down the mountainside. 'I wondered what on earth I was doing there,' she said afterwards.

It's a question that vexes many travellers. Paul Theroux, the American traveller, once got a lift from China to Tibet. It should have been a fairly calm journey but the car was driven by a nervous new driver who did not want to lose face. They crashed, but managed to continue. Theroux had a deep gash on his face, neckache, altitude sickness and a damaged wrist. He was thrown about in the back of the car and the driver was having a Chinese attack of the wobblies made worse by bouts of dizziness and sickness due to the height at which they were travelling. They had no spare wheel and petrol was low. After a while the road ran out and there was nothing in the bleak landscape but loose boulders, rocks, yaks and wild asses.

On that journey the romance of travel must have seemed dead, and yet, reading his account of the journey in *The Great Railway Bazaar*, the armchair traveller longs to experience being on the edge, as travellers often are. As Theroux commented, 'There is something about the very fact of survival that produces a greater vitality.' Not something that is likely to happen if you stay in the safety and lethargy of your armchair.

Safety and lethargy are two words barely acknowledged by the distinguished traveller, Wilfred Thesiger. He crossed one of the world's most dangerous places, the Empty Quarter in southern Arabia, twice. To explore the desert, Thesiger immersed himself in the Bedu way of life: he spoke Arabic, dressed and went barefoot as they did, and shared the extreme hardship of their existence. He gained their respect and they his. To know and understand the people among whom he lives is his way of travelling. 'In the desert', he wrote 'I had found all that I asked.' When he was forced to leave Arabia his sense of loss was enormous: 'As the plane . . . swung out to sea, I knew how it felt to go into exile.'

Six years later the traveller and writer Eric Newby had a chance meeting with Thesiger in the Hindu Kush. Thesiger invited him and his travelling companion to spend the night with his caravan. The ground was hard and peppered with rocks so Newby and his friend used their inflatable beds. Thesiger's response was typical of the man who had endured the searing heat, tongue-swelling thirst and bitter, skin-cracking cold of the desert: 'God, you must be a couple of pansies', he said.

As the unknown map of the world diminishes there are few places left for exploration as the Victorians understood it; most paths have been trodden before. But even the most well known of places is unknown to each traveller new to it. Colin Thubron illustrates this in a haunting story in *Behind The Wall*, an account of his travels in China. Walking south of the Great Wall he met a farm-worker who looked at an illustration of the Wall in Thubron's tourist map. The man had never seen it, although it lay only twenty miles to the north. He traced the drawing with his thumb saying 'Wonderful!' Then he went on his way. 'It could', wrote Thubron, 'have been the moon.'

Wilfred Thesiger with travelling companions in southern Arabia.

Opposite The Great Wall of China.

CHAPTER *3*

For All the People

THE SNORTING TRAIN sent steam
swirling through the buzzing crowd
of people as they swarmed from the
platform into the open wagons
drawn up at Leicester station. A
band played and onlookers waved
and cheered as men, women and
children wedged themselves into
the tub carriages and settled down for a good day
out. As far as they knew, these 570 people were off
to a temperance rally at Loughborough; most of
them were probably unaware that they were taking
part in an historical journey – Thomas Cook's first
excursion in 1841.

Nothing quite like it had happened before. Rail
travel was still new and Cook was the first person
to organize a group round fare – excursion rate for
'the enormous distance of eleven miles and back a
shilling, children half price'. The event was so
unusual that 'people crowded the streets, filled the
windows, covered the housetops, and cheered us
all along the line, with the heartiest welcome',
wrote Cook afterwards. Organized group travel
had begun in fine style.

Until that first excursion most travellers for
pleasure were the wealthy and the aristocracy who
travelled independently; less privileged people
travelled only through necessity. Even English
seaside resorts, which had been made popular
through royal patronage, saw relatively few
visitors. Thomas Cook's entrepreneurial spirit,
enthusiastic vision and social conscience changed
all that. 'God's green earth in all its fullness is for
the people' he proclaimed, and set about making
it possible with characteristic fervour.

At the time Cook was employed as secretary to
the South Midland Temperance Association, a
cause which he embraced with zeal, believing that
temperance could transform the lives of working·

Today, the InterCity 125 speeds along the Leicester to
Loughborough line.

Opposite Passengers on Thomas Cook's first excursion rode in open
carriages similar to these pulled by a replica of Stephenson's
Locomotion No. 1.

people. The idea for the first excursion had
flashed through his brain as he tramped across the
middle of England from Market Harborough to
Leicester on his way to attend a temperance
meeting. By the end of the next day he had
persuaded the Midland Counties Railway
Company to provide a special train and reduced
fares for his excursion. After that first success
Cook organized many more trips in the cause of
temperance, but in 1845 he put his organizational
skills to wider use and profit by arranging a public
excursion to Liverpool. Today we take organized
travel for granted but Cook's approach was
revolutionary. He went to Liverpool before the trip
and checked hotel accommodation and restaurants
to ensure that his 350 excursionists had the best
possible service. He then wrote *A Handbook of the
Trip to Liverpool* in which he gave every detail of the
excursion. It was probably the first guidebook of
its kind.

Other trips followed. Cook's pioneering
excursionists to Scotland were greeted with crowd-
lined streets, brass bands and cannon fire because
the tourist was still unusual enough to be an
entertaining curiosity. Cook was very much in
touch with what the public wanted and he
arranged many excursions to seaside towns
including Scarborough and Blackpool and resorts
such as Brighton and Hastings on the south coast
of England. Years spent as a printer had taught
Cook the value of advertising and his handbills
about the trips gave details of each town's
attractions, including the excellence of the shops.

Cook was an opportunist. He was quick to see
the possibilities for travel which the newly-
invented railways presented, and he reacted
speedily when the SS *Great Britain* ran aground in
Dundrum Bay by organizing an excursion to view
the stranded ship in 1847. National and
international events did not escape his
entrepreneurial skills. The Great Exhibition of
1851 brought him an excellent opportunity to
expand his business and he seized it with relish.
He did not make money, but he did make his
name by persuading a great many people to visit
the Exhibition with Cooks.

It was an amazing feat in the face of many
setbacks. The railways undercut his price and he
was forced to find many more passengers than he
had at first calculated. He set about it with
determination and enterprise. First he brought his
son, John Mason, aged seventeen, into the
business to help out in the crisis and together
father and son paraded through the streets of
Sheffield, Leeds, Derby and Bradford with a band,
making speeches about their trips to the Great
Exhibition. They had already set up Exhibition
clubs so that working men could pay in small
sums a week towards the total cost of an excursion

Opposite A handbill advertising one of Thomas Cook's excursions
to the Great Exhibition of 1851.

Thomas Cook (1808–1892). The founder of organized group travel,
and one of the world's largest travel companies. His vision broke
frontiers and opened up travel to ordinary people.

THE WONDER OF 1851!

FROM YORK
TO LONDON AND BACK FOR A CROWN.

THE MIDLAND RAILWAY COMPANY
Will continue to run

TWO TRAINS DAILY
(Excepted Sunday, when only one Train is available)

FOR THE GREAT EXHIBITION,
UNTIL SATURDAY, OCTOBER 11,

Without any Advance of }

RETURN SPECIAL TRAINS leave the Euston Station on MONDAYS, TUESDAYS, THURSDAYS, & SATURDAYS at 11 a.m., on WEDNESDAYS and FRIDAYS at 1 p.m., and EVERY NIGHT (Sundays excepted) at 9 p.m.

First and Second Class Tickets are available for returning any day (except Sunday) up to and including Monday, Oct. 20. Third Class Tickets issued before the 6th instant are available for 14 days, and all issued after the 6th are returnable any day up to Monday the 20th.

The Trains leave York at 9-40 a.m. every day except Sunday, and also every day, including Sunday, at 7-20 p.m.

Fares to London and Back!--

1st Class 15s. 2nd, 10s, 3rd, 5s.
The Midland is the only Company that runs Trains Daily at these Fares.
Ask for Midland Tickets!

Children above 3 and under 12 years of age, Half-price. Luggage allowed—112 lbs. to First Class, 100 lbs. to Second, and 56 lbs. to Third Class Passengers.

APPROVED LODGINGS, of all classes, are provided in London for Passengers by Midland Trains. The Agents will give Tickets of reference on application, without charge, and an Office is opened in London, at DONALD's WATERLOO DINING ROOMS, 14, Seymour-street, near Euston Station, where an agent is in regular attendance to conduct parties who go up unprepared with Lodgings.

The Managers have much pleasure in stating that the immense numbers who have travelled under their arrangements have been conducted in perfect safety—indeed in the history of the Midland Lines, *no accident, attended with personal injury, has ever happened to an Excursion Train.* In conducting the extraordinary traffic of this Great Occasion the first object is to ensure *safety*, and that object has hitherto been most happily achieved.

With the fullest confidence, inspired by past success, the Conductors have pleasure in urging those who have not yet visited the Exhibition, to avail themselves of the present facilities, and to improve the opportunity which will close on the 11th of October.

All communications respecting the Trains to be addressed to the Managers, for the Company,

**John Cuttle & John Calverley, Wakefield;
Thomas Cook, Leicester.**

October 2nd, 1851.

T. COOK, PRINTER, 28, GRANBY-STREET, LEICESTER.

ticket which included accommodation at the
Ranelagh Club – bed and a hearty Victorian
breakfast – for two shillings; the fare was five
shillings. Through their enthusiastic direct selling
methods Thomas and John Mason took 165,000
people to the Great Exhibition. It was a turning
point for the business and set Thomas Cook on

the road to opening up the world to men and
women who had not dreamed of travelling before.

Three years later Thomas Cook relinquished his
printing business and devoted all his attention to
being an excursion agent. In 1855 he took his first
party abroad to the Paris Exhibition and during
the same year organized and led a Grand Circular
Tour of Antwerp, Brussels, Waterloo, Cologne,
Frankfurt, Heidelberg, Baden Baden and Paris.
For centuries young bloods had been sent off by
indulgent parents to tour Europe in the hope that
they would return cultured, educated, their
manners refined and their address books packed
with useful contacts, but Cook's was the first
group tour of European countries organized by an
excursion agent. The following year his talent for
crowd control, grounded in his years as a Baptist

Excursionists arrive in Paris in 1861. The moment was captured
by an artist for the *Illustrated London News*.

preacher, was put to more commercial use when
Cook personally conducted 1,673 people to a
working-man's demonstration in Paris.

Thomas Cook's confidence and enthusiasm set
the pace. In 1863 he led a tour to Paris and
Switzerland; in 1864 he ventured to Italy with
parties of tourists. In that year Cook claimed that
he had one million clients and the business was
stable enough for him to settle clients' bills, but
he was not actually running inclusive tours yet.
The following year Cook made a bold step to
expand and consolidate his business: he opened
an office in London, at 98 Fleet Street, which was
run by his son, John Mason.

Did Cook achieve all this without competition,
was he the only excursion agent in business in the
second half of the nineteenth century? The
Victorian entrepreneurs did not miss the
extraordinary opportunities offered by the
business of travel and Cook and his descendants
had many rivals who gave them keen competition.
One was Henry Gaze, who had begun tours as
early as 1844 with a trip from London to Boulogne
and Paris, and took a party to view the battlefields
of Waterloo in 1854. At first Cook viewed this
rival with gentlemanly magnanimity. When Gaze
published a guidebook to Switzerland Cook
recommended it saying 'the book is written in
good style, and displays the spirit of energy, self
denial, and perseverance that should characterise
Alpine travellers'. But the spirit of goodwill did
not last long and Gaze was soon claiming that
Cook was copying his ideas. Rivalry persisted
through the 1860s and '70s and in 1881 Gaze
produced a pamphlet which claimed that certain
companies were apt to 'monopolise powers which
are the property of all Tourist Agents, and in the
development of which we ourselves have borne so
important a part'. But after 1902, nothing more
was heard of Henry Gaze.

The British were the pioneers of organized
travel and several companies followed the example
of Cook and Gaze. Many of them had educational
or philanthropic aims. The Polytechnic Touring
Association which began in 1888 gave students of
the London Polytechnic a chance to travel. The
emphasis of their tours was on education and
recreation for students and by the 1890s they were
offering cruises to Norway for eight guineas.
Cycling was the craze of the era and The Cycling
Travellers' Club organized their first tour to the
Continent in 1879. The Workers' Travel
Association was set up to give workers the
opportunity to travel; it began in a modest way
but by the 1950s had become a worldwide
organization.

Henry Lunn, one of the major figures of the
early days of organized travel, was also inspired by
high ideals. He was the editor of the *Review of*

Cook's London office in Fleet Street, on the corner of Ludgate
Circus, opened in 1865.

Churches and the first tour which he organized was in 1893 when he took a party of 450 people to Rome for Easter. At the time Cook was concentrating on smaller, more select parties which left a gap in the market for larger tours. Henry Lunn seized the opportunity and organized educational cruises aboard the steam yacht

A party of sightseers leaves the American Express Office at 55, Charlottenstrasse, Berlin, in 1913.

Argonaut to the Greek islands to visit, as the advertising put it: 'ground immortalised by the poetry of Sophocles, the eloquence of Demosthenes, and the missionary zeal of St Paul . . . To anyone with the requisite classical training . . . this must be a delightful Easter holiday . . . shared with kindred spirits.' Lunn was also responsible for popularizing winter sports outside Scandinavia. In 1902 he founded the Public Schools Alpine Sports Club and although this was snobbishly restricted to those who had been to a British public school, the club was instrumental in establishing winter sports as a popular type of holiday. Lunn's travel business was eventually amalgamated with the Polytechnic Touring Association to form Lunn Poly in the 1960s.

There was a rival from across the Atlantic too. The American Express Company was founded in 1850, primarily to carry mail, gold bullion and passengers, but it gradually moved into shipping and in the 1890s set up offices in Europe's major ports handling freight bound for the United States. There were already American tourists visiting Europe whose lives were made easier by the newly-patented American Express 'Travelers Cheque'. Many of them were students who worked their passage to Liverpool as cattlemen aboard the cattle-steamers before the days of full-scale refrigeration, and used the Liverpool office to cash their generous allowances. Some executives of the company wanted to expand into the travel business, but in 1900 the testy head of American Express, James Congdell Fargo, was still adamantly against it, 'I will not have gangs of trippers starting off in charabancs from in front of our offices the way they do from Cooks', he stormed. 'We will cash their Travelers Cheques and give them free advice. That's all . . .' He did not win: the executive in charge of setting up the European offices was the dynamic ex-sheriff of Caribou, Idaho, named William Swift Daliba, who could toss a silver dollar in the air and plug it with his six-gun. Daliba's enterprise triumphed and a photograph of 1913 shows an American Express charabanc, loaded with tourists, leaving the company's Berlin office on a sightseeing trip. Today American Express is one of the largest travel companies in the world.

Unperturbed by the excellence of their rivals, the formidable Cook family – Thomas senior, John Mason and his sons Ernest, Frank and young Thomas – continued to forge innovations for the travel business throughout the second half of the nineteenth century. In 1851 Thomas started the first travel magazine: *The Excursionist* (renamed *The Traveller's Gazette* in 1903), containing details of Cook's forthcoming excursions, advice to travellers, and articles and reports about the trips. It was published regularly for almost a century and appeared in twelve editions and seven languages.

All through the American Civil War Thomas Cook watched the great North American continent, which was then virgin territory untrampled by the feet of British tourists, with a covetous eye. As soon as the war was over in 1865 Thomas crossed the Atlantic and reconnoitred the New World. The following year a Cook's tour was the very first group of European tourists to set foot in America. Led by John Mason they visited, among other places, New York, Washington, Niagara, Chicago, the Mammoth Caves of Kentucky and, rather gruesomely, the recently deserted battlefields of Virginia where they saw 'skulls, arms and legs all bleaching in the sun'. The excursion party of thirty travelled 10,500 miles in nine weeks with John Mason overseeing all the arrangements, dealing with over a hundred railway and steamboat officials and lamenting the

John Mason Cook with his wife Emma, and son Frank, who later ran Cook's Middle East business from the Cairo office.

'lightening' steamboats and trains which travelled at fifteen miles per hour. 'I flatter myself', he wrote on the evening after he arrived home, 'that even our American friends must admit that nobody but a "Britisher" would have been able to successfully cope with such difficulties.'

British phlegm and perseverance carried the

Opposite Poster advertising Cook's Nile cruises.

A Cook caravan pauses for a photograph beside their camp in the Middle East in the last quarter of the nineteenth century.

Cooks through many difficult situations. Their arrangements and business deals were an astonishing feat made, as they were, without the benefit of modern technology – no last minute checks on the computer or facsimile confirmations, no satellites to speed international communications. John Mason Cook turned out to be an even more successful businessman than his father (which caused a considerable amount of friction between father and son); his acumen, energy and determination swept the company, which was already successful, to international recognition and the name of Cook became synonymous with travel worldwide.

All this was achieved in the face of difficulties which deterred men with less gusto than Thomas and John Mason. There were no hotels in the Holy Land when Thomas accompanied his first tour there in 1868, so the whole Cook's party of sixty people became a vast caravan, accompanied by sixty-five horses, eighty-seven pack mules, tents,

Inside, the tents were furnished as comfortably as possible: iron bedsteads and hot water were provided for Cook's tourists.

COOK'S NILE SERVICE.

P. S. "Rameses the Great"

beds and field kitchens to prepare gargantuan
Victorian breakfasts of boiled eggs followed by
chicken and cutlets, and dinners of seven courses
including wild boar and mutton. To attend the
travellers there were servants, muleteers, guides,
and guards to deter marauding bandits. Dressed
for any eventuality the tourists peer from formal

Nineteenth-century tourists brave the camel's hump.

photographs, the men wearing waistcoats, ties,
wing collars, jackets, the women in high necked
blouses and long skirts, with elaborate hats pinned
firmly to their heads. Keeping up appearances was
important. When one of the party, a Mrs Samuels,
died on the trip, Cook diplomatically disguised
the fact from the Arabs and, pretending that she
was ill, packed up her body and had it carried in a
palanquin until a suitable burial could be
arranged.

After the opening of the Suez Canal in 1869, Egypt became an exotic magnet for the Victorian tourist. John Mason Cook saw the potential of Egypt's tourist industry in her magnificent antiquities and the majestic River Nile, and under his dynamic leadership the Egyptian tourist industry was born. Cook's monopoly of the

One of Cook's Nile steamers. Cook was appointed agent for Nile passenger traffic by the Khedive of Egypt in 1870 and eventually had a fleet of seventeen large vessels and about thirty-three smaller dahabeeyahs and pinnaces.

industry had such a grip that Arabs referred to tourists as 'Cookii' rather than travellers.

Before Cook's tours of Egypt, Victorian travellers hired their own boats to travel up the Nile. They were so verminous that early guidebooks such as Murray's advised that they should be sunk as soon as they were hired to get rid of rats, mice and scorpions. Cook eventually created his own fleet of floating palaces to carry the 'Cookii' down the Nile. They were built in Scotland and transported in sections to Egypt where they were assembled in Cook's own shipyard at Boulac. Life on board these opulent ships was claimed by one tourist to be 'the perfection of human existence': electric light, carpets, libraries, ladies' saloons, gleaming brass, and white-robed servants with red tarbooshes to provide excellent service. John Mason Cook organized a series of market gardens along the Nile to provide his ships with fresh vegetables. His standards were exacting. When one of the dragomen did not perform to perfection, John Mason tossed him overboard into the brown waters of the Nile and took the helm himself. The Sphinx, said Victorian tourists, broke her eternal silence to congratulate Cook on his Nile cruises.

Nile boatman.

Overleaf The River Nile.

But tourism had its detractors. Amelia Edwards, travelling independently up the Nile in 1873, recorded: 'the people in dahabeeyahs [hired boats] despise Cook's tourists.' The sinking heart experienced by today's independent traveller at the sight of a coach disgorging tourists to teeter round the ancient temples of Egypt on white high

heels, or garlanded with the entire contents of a photographic shop, ready to snap everything in sight, is not new.

In nineteenth-century Europe things were no better: 'These devil's dust tourists have spread over Europe injuring our credit and damaging our character. Their gross ignorance is the very smallest of their sins . . . anything so uncouth I never saw before . . .' wrote the British Consul at La Spezia, Italy, under the *nom de plume* Cornelius O'Dowd. Fanny Kemble, the Victorian actress, thought that tourism had ruined Switzerland, that its hotels had become like gin palaces and that the effect of special tourist events amid the sublime scenery was very vulgar: '. . . bread and butter,

Victorian tourists pose at the foot of one of the great pyramids. Egypt became a popular tourist destination in the nineteenth century and continues to attract many visitors.

and pâté de foie gras, and marmalade and jam, and caviare, one on top of the other'. It seems that there are some minds which travel will never broaden: vulgarity, riotous behaviour, high spirits and horseplay have scandalized the establishment since the birth of tourism – the 1980s Costa Brava lager lout had his parallel in the Victorian excursionist. Tourists on the Riviera in the 1930s moved Beverly Nichols to desperation: 'Ye Gods, the people!', he wrote, 'Drunken, debauched, heartless, of an incredible vulgarity – swooping, screaming, racketing.'

When Thomas Cook died at the age of eighty-four in 1892 *The Times* obituary was fulsome in the praise of his achievements, but bemoaned the fact that he could not change the character of the average tourist:

> The world is not altogether reformed by cheap tours, nor is the inherent vulgarity of the British Philistine going to be eradicated by sending him with a through ticket and a bundle of hotel coupons to Egypt and the Holy Land. . . . If only Messrs Cook could guarantee a benefit to mind and manners as easily as they can guarantee a comfortable journey!

Newspapers and periodicals of the time, such as *Punch* and the *Illustrated London News*, were full of cartoons and illustrations of the despised tourist.

But the humorist Jerome K. Jerome could find nothing amusing to write about English-speaking tourists of the 1890s: '. . . taken as a whole, a most disagreeable contingent. . . . The women are the most objectionable. . . . The average female English or American Tourist is rude and self-assertive while at the same time ridiculously helpless and awkward. She is intensely selfish, utterly inconsiderate of others; everlastingly complaining, and, in herself, drearily uninteresting.'

Thomas Cook would have disagreed vehemently with this point of view. He was not a lady's man in the accepted sense, rather he championed and encouraged single women to travel at a time when it was still considered bad form for a respectable young lady to take a shopping trip to London unchaperoned, let alone visit the Continent. Emancipation for women was beginning to rumble and Cook may have embraced the idea, but, being a shrewd opportunist, it is more likely that he saw potential customers among women who were striving for more freedom. Whatever the motives, Cook played an important role in enabling middle-class women to travel for pleasure. Until his organized excursions, travel was considered far too dangerous a pastime for most women. When taking a train journey women were advised to equip themselves with the largest hat-pin they

Complaints about the behaviour of some tourists began as early as the 1850s. Their vulgarity, loudness and lack of manners scandalized their hosts.

The woman traveller featured in many travel magazines.

could find and if travelling by night, or through a
tunnel, they were to sit bolt upright, hat-pin
clenched between the teeth in case of attack.

With Cook, women felt safe. Matilda Lincolne,
who with her three sisters went on Cook's first
overseas tour (Belgium, France and Germany) in
1855, wrote in her journal:

Tourists observe the niceties of correct dress while viewing the
Matterhorn.

Many of our friends thought us too independent
and adventurous to leave the shores of old
England, and thus plunge into foreign countries
not beneath Victoria's sway, with no protecting
relatives, but we can only say that we hope this
will not be our last excursion of this kind. We
could venture anywhere with such a guide and
guardian as Mr Cook for there was not one of
our party but felt perfectly safe when under his
care.

Matilda was the first of many. Eventually the
majority of Cook's excursionists were women; they
climbed the Alps, negotiated glaciers, scrambled
up the Pyramids and crossed deserts, dressed
always as if they were about to take afternoon tea
with the vicar. Cook revelled in their spirit and
tenacity and after a camping tour to the Holy
Land in 1869 he wrote:

The results of this tour, so far as the ladies of
the party were concerned, tended to confirm all
my previous impressions of their valour and
vigour, and also to the strengthening of my
determination never to undertake or propose

any arrangement from which the ladies must of necessity be excluded.

Cook published books and pamphlets of advice to women travellers which contained every detail of suitable dress – even to a preference for button, rather than elastic-sided boots, which made ankles

THE REGISTERED
ASHANTEE POCKET HAMMOCK.
(IMPROVED PATTERN)

As supplied to H.R.H. the Prince of Wales, and to Government for the Ashantee Expedition.

(Gold Medal at International Horticultural Exhibition at Oporto, Portugal, July, 1877.

It makes a most luxurious Couch, Seat, &c., in the GARDEN, THE WOODS, ON BOARD SHIP, or ANYWHERE INDOORS, and can be slung in a few minutes wherever the simplest means of support exist. Tourists, Sportsmen, and Travellers generally will find it a source of great comfort and enjoyment. Weighs from 1½ lb. upwards, and will bear the weight of half a dozen adult persons. A good Bed can be easily improvised with it in a full hotel or house.

Sir Garnet Wolseley says, "It proved most comfortable for travelling in during the campaign."

HAMMOCK PACKED IN CASE WITH STRAP TO HANG OVER SHOULDER. SIZE OF PARCEL 10 × 5 TO 13 × 5 IN. WEIGHT FROM 1½ lb TO 4 lbs

Mr. H. M. Stanley, of African renown, says, "Nothing more portable, yet so efficient and perfect for its purpose, could be invented or manufactured."

See also Mr. STANLEY's book, "Through the Dark Continent," Vol. I. page 82.

Dr. Russell, Special *Times* Correspondent, accompanying His Royal Highness the Prince of Wales during his Indian journey, states a medical officer of the Army of high reputation, gives a very favourable account of Seydel's patent hammocks for the transport of sick and wounded in railway carriages, to which we add our testimony to their extreme comfort and convenience for persons in sound health camping out or engaged in voyages by land or sea. They are very portable and very light and strong, and can be easily fixed in a room or out of doors. *They were used on board the "Serapis" by the Royal suite, and gave the greatest satisfaction.*

PRICES (including neat Case, Ropes, Screw-hooks, and Large Illustrated Sheet)—
No. 1, the original "Ashantee," total length 10 feet, available length 6 feet ....10s. 6d. Other Sorts—No. 2, 12s.; No. 3, 15s.; No. 5, 18s.; No. 6, 21s.; No. 40, Silk, 63s.; No. 50, Silk, 105s. Slinging Apparatus (in Canvas Bag), including pair of Spreading Sticks, replacing Trees, Ash Wood, 7s. 6d Hickory Wood, 9s. Spreading Sticks, only, 1s. per pair; very useful. Tent Umbrellas, 9s. 6d. each.

Sole Manufacturers:

 SEYDEL & CO., 7½, St. Mary's Row, Birmingham.
London Wholesale Agents:
MESSRS. J. AND T. BAYLEY, 1, COUSIN LANE, E.C.

Retailed by Outfitters, Tent and Garden Furniture Dealers, India Rubber Warehouses, Gunmakers, Travelling Requisite, Fishing Tackle, Cricket Goods Dealers, &c.

swell on lengthy tours of museums, cathedrals and ruins. Other publications followed his example. *The Girl's Own Paper* of 1890 published intimidating lists of the clothes essential for travelling which included twenty dresses, as many skirts and high necked blouses, jackets to match everything, coats, cloaks, hats, gloves, handkerchiefs and veils. In addition:

An indiarubber folding bath, an Etna or small spirit kettle, and a bottle of spirits; some tea and a little sugar; a bath towel or two; an air cushion, or a pillow; a small drinking-cup and flask; soap; a pot of Leibig or Bovril; matches and candles; medicine; some potted meat for sandwiches; insect powder and mosquito

Advertisements in travel magazines offered every kind of aid to the traveller, including a bag complete with pulley for escape.

"KIT BAG ESCAPE."

netting; vaseline, lipsalve, camphor, sal volatile, seidlitz powders, mustard leaves, chlorodyne, and eau de cologne.

The young female beast of burden could have added the indispensible portable door-lock, guaranteed to keep undesirables out of the flimsiest room, which was advertised in Cook's *Excursionist*.

'The bicycle is the greatest emancipator for woman extant . . .' exclaimed a 'lady-writer' in 1901. But in *The Girl's Own Paper* of the same year the resident doctor 'Medicus' replied:

It sounds to a man's understanding as if women had hitherto been kept in disagreeable subjection to the stronger and sterner sex. I don't think any woman, unless an old maid, hankers after emancipation of that sort, which seems to mean that, mounted on her bike, a girl can ride away anywhere and do anything all alone, without either male friend or chaperone, that she can guide and protect herself and be as free and easy as the wind. . . . No girls, don't let's have too much of that emancipation business. Better to be loved and admired by a true and good man than be 'emancipated'.

'Medicus' was a bit behind the times for Cooks, who, building on the work of their founder, had seized on the cycling craze of the 1890s and advertised cycling tours on the Continent which were especially aimed at single women. Cooks did, however, nod to convention and only admitted single women to the tour if they were accompanied by a relative or friend. They also acknowledged the amount of luggage deemed necessary and organized baggage transport to take trunks from hotel to hotel while the healthy cyclist rode unencumbered for twenty to fifty miles a day.

Women's new-found physical freedom extended to other outdoor activities, particularly winter sports. Cooks were not the instigators of winter sports holidays, that was the achievement of Henry Lunn, but they were the champions of winter sports for women. Many of their posters from the early 1900s through to the 1920s show young women skiing, skating and tobogganing, and women took to the slopes of Grindelwald, St Moritz and those of less fashionable and more affordable resorts, with a zest which matched the mountain air, while their American sisters slid, swooped and glided down the slopes and across the ponds of Vermont or the Rockies. Women from both sides of the Atlantic continued to push back the frontiers of travel throughout the twentieth century. They took to each new form of transport enthusiastically, motoring across Europe and the States in the twenties and taking to the air in the thirties.

A roadside break for a cigarette and a bike check, 1890s.
Inset The right clothes for the occasion, 1899.

Opposite Woman cyclist of 1898 sporting the latest in cycling fashion.

Winter Sport
Arrangements.

THOS. COOK & SON.

Thomas Cook's achievement was, as *The Times* said in his obituary, to 'organise travel as it was never organised before'. Early Victorian travellers could not be certain of a clean bed and a meal in a hotel of their choice, nor of obtaining train tickets on the complex European rail network. Cook and his son, John Mason, changed all that. They set up a system of hotel coupons (1867), through rail tickets, international ship and rail timetables, and guidebooks, and between 1873 and 1874 they introduced the Circular Note, forerunner of the travellers cheque. The inclusive tour, in which every item of travel arrangement was paid for in advance, was Thomas Cook's invention. Too many Cooks did not spoil the travellers' broth and by the end of the nineteenth century Cooks had offices across Europe and America, Australia and New Zealand, Canada, the Middle East and India.

Such international fame and popular appeal guaranteed that the ubiquitous 'man from Cooks' entered the English language, that songs about Cook's tours were published and sung around the piano of the Victorian parlour and that Thomas Cook had a cocktail named after him – the Cooktail. John Mason died in 1899 at the early age of sixty-four. He had seemed indefatigable; his diaries reveal that between 1865 and 1870 he had travelled at least forty-two thousand miles per year, but he died only seven years after his father, leaving the business in the capable hands of his sons Ernest, Frank and Tom.

In addition to middle-class tourists, Cook's facilities and efficiency attracted illustrious clients who included most of the British royal family, the Kaiser, the Czar and many European aristocrats, politicians (including Gladstone), bishops and archbishops, industrialists like Krupp, and Indian princes who felt they could entrust whole entourages – wives, children, advisers, court officials, servants, elephants, tigers and artillery – to Cook's care when they visited Britain to celebrate Victoria's Jubilee.

Writers like Kipling, Oscar Wilde and H. Rider Haggard found unique words of praise. 'They wire money like angels' said Wilde. Haggard recounted the power of Cook's name in the only travel book he wrote. While waiting in wind and rain to board a ship in Haifa the hapless passengers who included Haggard were hassled by a Turkish official:

Cook, Cook, Cook! we croaked in deprecatory tones as one by one we crept past him cowed and cold, fearing that he might invent some pretext to detain us . . . we hurried to bring to his notice the only name which seems to have power in Syria, that famous name of the hydra-headed, the indispensible, the world-wide Cook.

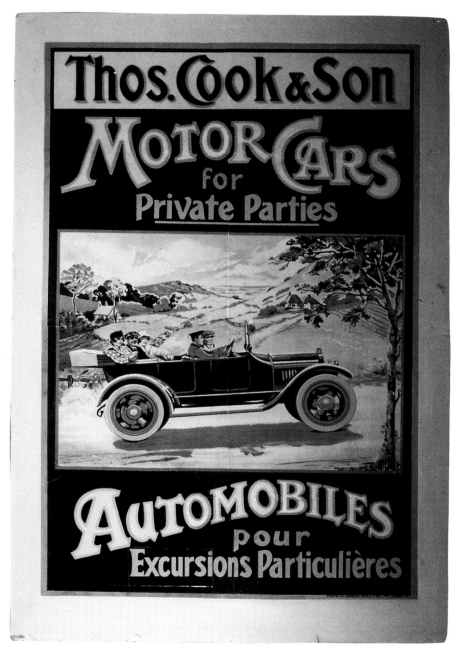

A bilingual poster advertising motor cars for private hire. Touring on the Riviera was a must for the well-to-do of the 1920s and '30s.

Opposite Thomas Cook led the way in popularizing winter sports for women: the cover of a Cook's winter sports brochure for the 1911–12 season.

They were allowed to board without further delay.

'. . . to be on the Riviera without a motor car is a condition we do not care to imagine', reported *Vogue* in the 1920s. The First World War was over and Europe was once again open for pleasure. The smart set took to motoring and to France,

Bathing belles of the 1920s.

especially the Riviera, intent on forgetting the war. Having a spiffingly good time on the French and Italian beaches of the Mediterranean was the summer order of the decade, although as Noel Coward caustically commented, some would-be hedonists spent hours '. . . squabbling viciously and brushing flakes of their own sun-scorched flesh from the table.'

Motoring was the thing and the newly-built military roads which criss-crossed Europe carried affluent motorists in search of the pleasure and adventure of travelling. Lord Cardigan found it in the Balkans where proper roads petered out and pot-hole dodging enlivened the journey. There were no signposts and maps were not to be

trusted, but the greatest hazard he encountered
was a swarm of locusts which had taken
possession of five miles of the road. 'Driving
through a locust swarm is a revolting experience'
he wrote. 'The car leaves behind it two long trails
of squashy corpses, the tyres and wheels become
encrusted with them, while the running boards are

Motoring gave the affluent new opportunities for travel and leisure
in the 1920s: a picnic in 1922.

soon black with those that still live and crawl.' In
the middle of the chaos the unfortunate earl's car
got a puncture; sorting that out was an
unspeakable experience.

While Lord Cardigan was changing his wheel
among the heaving insects in the Greek
mountains, most people in Europe and America
stayed at home. The Victorians, including Thomas
Cook, saw travel as 'improving'. Even by 1920, the
concept of a holiday taken purely for sybaritic
enjoyment was still something many people
wrestled with. Only the affluent could afford to
take vacations or to travel abroad because holidays
with pay were not mandatory in the 1920s. The
British had to wait until the end of the 1930s for

that luxury. If they could afford to take a holiday at all, the working people of Britain went on day trips to the seaside, while the Americans explored their vast country.

The late twenties and early thirties saw the proliferation of two forms of travel: the fastest – air travel, and the most leisurely – cruising. Air travel grew rapidly: the first Pan Am passenger flight was on 18 January 1928, although the first commercial passenger flights had been in German *Zeppelins* before the First World War, and French and British airlines had begun by the early 1920s. The development of commercial airlines had an immense impact on travel and in the thirties they really began to take off.

'Cruising' according to a postcard written by twenty-one-year-old Dorothea Whitcombe in 1932 'is the only way to travel.' A lot of other people in the thirties agreed: in the early years of the decade over two hundred cruises a year left British ports, and there were others leaving Continental and American ports too. *Vogue* assured its readers that 'everyone goes cruising and the trouble is not to find a cruise but to choose from the numberless, almost equally alluring cruises that are most suited to one's particular fancy'. In 1934, P & O, Cunard, Blue Star, Orient and Royal Mail took passengers as far afield as Japan, Australia, and Hawaii. And they were not all billionaires: it was possible to take a ten day cruise to North Africa for £9.

Although it reached its peak of popularity in the 1930s, cruising had begun in about 1844 when P & O's cruise through the Mediterranean was described by the writer William Makepeace Thackeray, and Mark Twain wrote about a cruise of 1868 from New York to the Mediterranean in his book *Innocents Abroad*. The very first cruise around the world in one ship was organized by American Express who chartered the *Laconia* in 1922.

At the beginning of the thirties it must have seemed as if the world was opening up at an astonishing rate, but by the end of the decade it had closed to all but those on active military service. Ironically the Second World War enabled many people who had not had the opportunity to travel to see something of other countries. Cooks organized tours for servicemen and women on leave included a guided tour of the casbah in Algiers which was accompanied by an armed American guard.

Petrol rationing, restricted travel, limited travel allowances, the Iron Curtain, expensive air travel and ships still commandeered, made travel in the immediate post-war period seem a bleak prospect. But all that changed at a phenomenal pace. In Britain the Holidays with Pay Act of 1938 had, by the end of the war, freed between fourteen and

Cruising is still popular: a cruise ship in the warm waters of St Lucia. *Inset* Poster advertising Cooks pleasure cruises.

BOURNEMOUTH
& WEYMOUTH
PASSENGERS
HOLDING SEAT
RESERVATIONS

FOR 9·24 TRAIN

PLEASE ASSEMBLE
OTHER SIDE
OF THIS BOARD

ENQUIRIES

fifteen million people to take paid holidays. Within two years the volume of travel was higher practically everywhere in the world than it had been before the war. From then on, throughout the fifties, it doubled itself every five years. The travel boom had begun.

More people owned motor cars than previously:

The rail excursion, popularized by Thomas Cook during the nineteenth century, continued into the twentieth: jaunty boaters adorn Londoners bound for the seaside, Waterloo station, May 1912. *Inset* Porter, G.C. Railway, London, 1907.

by 1956 there was one car for every three people in the United States; in France and Britain the figure was one for every thirteen people. So travelling by car became popular. Coach tours proliferated and so did specially-chartered trains to take holiday-makers to destinations in their own countries or abroad. The major increase was in air travel. Just before the war about a hundred thousand passengers flew from Britain to the Continent and they were mostly businessmen, not tourists. Until 1939 there was no regular air service between Britain and the United States. By 1949 the world's airlines had carried over twenty million paying passengers, by 1956 the figure had reached over sixty million and it was estimated

Opposite Waiting for the train, bank holiday in England, 1950s.

that 90 per cent of the world's land surface could be reached by the traveller.

And it was travellers, not tourists, who did most of the travelling. Although Thomas Cook had started the package tour to enable the masses to travel, it was still beyond the reach of most people's pockets. The pioneer of the beach

Ranked on crowded beaches, tourists soak up the sun in Italy.

package holiday was a young Russian immigrant to Britain called Vladimir Raitz, who launched a daring air package experiment in the late forties.

A war surplus Douglas DC9 aircraft and tents in Corsica were the ingredients of Raitz's first package holiday. For £35 10s 0d he offered a return air fare and a camping holiday in the Corsican sunshine. The experiment worked and by 1954 Raitz's Horizon Holidays had taken off and by the end of the fifties he was offering holidays on the Costa Brava, the Costa del Sol, in Portugal, Minorca and Tangiers.

Row upon row of sunburnt bodies, oiled like sardines, covered the beaches of Spanish resorts by the early 1970s. All through the 1960s the package holiday market had grown and by the early 1970s they accounted for nearly half of all overseas travel. Fierce competition between the major tour operators in Britain, Germany and

Scandinavia produced advantageous deals with airlines and hotels; there were better and more economical aircraft, and less financial restrictions, all of which produced cheaper holidays. Many people who had never been abroad before were happy to let the tour operator take the strain and send them off on holidays where everything was organized for them.

There were, of course, plenty of people who did not view catching a plane at the shriek of dawn, fighting for a patch of sand big enough to spread a handkerchief, suffering appalling hangovers from over-indulgence in Spanish 'champagne', and arriving home burnt to a painful scarlet wearing a ridiculous hat and clutching a straw donkey too big to stand on the television, as travel. They continued to make their own arrangements. Young people of the late sixties and early seventies who were more affluent, had more time and had grown up with an expectation of seeing more of the world, were able to travel far more easily than previous generations. Some travelled east following the hippy trail to India and Nepal in search of the meaning of life. Others, such as young Australians and New Zealanders, travelled west to arrive in the squalor of Earl's Court, London. From Mars it must have looked as if opposing armies of ants were on the move. From 1977, if they wanted to cross the Atlantic cheaply, they turned to Freddie Laker.

To get a ticket on Laker's Skytrain in the summer of 1978 (£59 one way, available only on day of flight) you had to join a queue 2,000 people long. Sometimes the wait to reach the ticket office in London's Victoria Station took five days so the queuers built themselves shelters of cardboard, plastic sacks and string, turning the queue into a shanty town wittily christened 'Lakerville' by its occupants. But the reward was the cheapest transatlantic air ticket available.

Sir Freddie Laker was the entrepreneurial fox who cheekily jumped into the airlines' broiler house and mightily ruffled their wings. He believed that there was a market for very cheap tickets. His idea was simple: seats on Skytrain were not bookable in advance, they had to be bought on the day of travel in New York, London, or later San Francisco, and food on the flight had to be paid for. Laker took on the airlines' cartel which held ticket prices high and broke it single-handed. Skytrain was so successful that the other airlines had to follow suit and offer passengers cheaper fares. Laker was the people's friend and knighted for his achievements, but the airlines did not forgive his cheek and by 1982 Laker was finished. Many believe that his fall was brought about by rivals.

'The Silk Road'; 'China the Beautiful'; 'The Palaces of Rajasthan'; 'The Magic of India'; 'Across

Opposite Colour pervades everyday life in Rajasthan.

The Ganges: sacred river of Hindus. *Inset* A makeshift shelter in Lakerville. Young people queue for Laker airline tickets in London, 1978.

INDIA

24/9/35 12,000

the Roof of the World' read the travel brochures of the 1980s. The package tour was not dead, it had gone up market and further afield. Of course, if you were a *Vogue* reader with a purse to match, you would have been urged to visit such places in the 1970s, but where the rich (or adventurous) manage to travel independently, the package

The mountains of Guilin, inspiration of poets and painters, and mecca of travellers in China. *Inset* Colossal stone Buddha, Thailand.

holiday-maker reaches a decade later and, just as Thomas Cook had envisaged, the inclusive tour enables more people to travel to far-flung destinations.

By the beginning of the present decade tourism was very big business indeed. The wealthy nations of the world generate most of the tourists – the Japanese, Germans, Americans, Scandinavians and British are among the most widely travelled. For some the trend of the 1990s is to move away from package holidays towards the individual tour where travel agents help the client to arrange a personal itinerary. Others make their own arrangements. In 1927, the travel writer Robert Byron wrote 'It is often remarked that the Twentieth Century is an age of easy travel. In fact, there is scarcely any more travelling to be done.' Perhaps not for a seasoned traveller like Byron, but for most people there are still thousands of miles to cover and hundreds of countries to explore.

Opposite Cooks poster, 1935: India still beckons.

CHAPTER *4*

By Land, Sea and Air

Just As The Panting Cyclist drew ahead of the London to St Alban's coach the guard hurled an iron ball on a rope into the spokes of the bicycle wheel and felled the rider. The coachman reined in his horses, leapt into the road and, seizing the sprawling cyclist, beat him soundly with his whip for having the temerity to overtake the coach. The year was 1876 and the coachman was later fined for his behaviour, but the incident illustrates the reactionary's response to new forms of transport. In 1869, the year that bicycles were first manufactured in Britain, *The Times* had called cyclists 'A New Terror to the Streets'. When the Duke of Wellington was confronted by the realities of the steam locomotive he responded: 'I see no reason to suppose that these machines will ever force themselves into general use.'

The grand old duke was wrong of course. The train revolutionized not only the means of transport but also people's ideas and expectations about travel. Not that the beginnings of rail travel were auspicious. When the American train, the 'De Witt Clinton', clattered along the rails in 1831 the good citizens of Albany, proud to be its first passengers, were showered with burning embers from the tall funnel of the locomotive. At the first watering place they jumped from the open wagons and rushed to douse their burning clothes. Jumping from moving trains was the cause of many accidents in the early days of railways. Passengers just did not realize how fast trains travelled and contemporary reports list serious injuries and fatalities sustained when people leapt off trains to retrieve hats or umbrellas. People were run over by trains because they would stretch themselves out on the rails for a quick

The railroads began to open up America during the 1830s: the 'De Witt Clinton', one of the most historic locomotives on the Mohawk and Hudson Railroad, 1831.

Opposite An early Royal Mail shipping line poster.

nap, or because they were drunk. And many had
their skulls smashed when riding on top of a
carriage because they 'came into collision with a
bridge'.

George Stephenson himself drove the first
passenger train on Tuesday 27 September 1825.
Many of those who rode along the line from

An early American locomotive.

Stockton to Darlington on that day 'did not the
night before sleep a wink. . . . The happy faces of
many, the vacant stare of astonishment of others,
and the alarm depicted on the countenance of
some, gave variety to the picture', was the scene
set by an onlooker. Five years later the actress
Fanny Kemble sat beside Stephenson on a trial
trip on the Liverpool to Manchester railway in
1830. She found him a 'rather stern-featured man',
with a strong Northumbrian accent and seems to
have preferred the 'Rocket' which she described as
'This snorting little animal, which I felt inclined
to pat . . .' and so ranks among the first to fall
under the spell of the steam locomotive. She
wrote, 'You can't imagine how strange it seemed
to be journeying thus, without any visible cause
for progress other than the magical machine, with
its flying white breath and rhythmical, unvarying
pace. . . .'

The train provided cheap travel for the masses. Before Trevithick's invention and Stephenson's vision and tenacity, the furthest most people travelled from home was the next village or the nearest town on market day. Not only did the train travel fast, it spread fast and soon the world was opening up at a pace not previously imagined. By the time Charles Dickens got there in 1842, trains were already careering through America:

> . . . on, on, on tears the mad dragon of an engine . . . scattering in all directions a shower of burning sparks from its wood fire; screeching, hissing, yelling, panting; until at last the thirsty monster stops beneath a covered way to drink . . . and you have time to breathe again.

Thomas Cook was one of the first entrepreneurs to see the huge possibilities of rail travel and in 1844, after the success of his early excursions, he pronounced that he wanted 'railways for the millions'.

Railways for the millions did not mean luxury. Even on long journeys early trains had no corridors, lavatories, dining cars or heating. John Gadsby who travelled across France in 1855 found that he needed two greatcoats and a large travelling wrapper to keep himself warm even though the carriage was supplied with hot foot-warmers which were renewed at certain stops along the route. Mark Twain, the American writer, found European trains primitive after his native ones: 'The conductor locks you in when the train starts; there is no water to drink in the car, there is no heating apparatus . . . they have not that culmination of all charity and human kindness, a sleeping car . . . .' That particular luxury did not appear until M. Georges Nagelmackers had copied Mr Pullman and introduced them in 1883, and even then they were for the rich who could afford to travel on the 'Orient Express'.

North America became the first continent to have a rail line from coast to coast when the Central Pacific met the Union Pacific in May 1869. By the 1870s New York had an ingenious solution to its transport problems: the elevated railway, Third Avenue, New York, 1879.

Luxury for first class travellers: a sleeping car attendant delivers hot water bottles on the London-to-Inverness Express, January 1935. *Left* The uneven struggle to read a newspaper on a train dates from the early days of rail travel.

To prevent starvation on more plebian trains, passengers had to take all their food with them or leap from the train the moment it drew into a station and rush for the buffet. The ensuing chaos was almost life-threatening and the timid always ran the risk of reboarding without food or being left behind when the train steamed out. The great Indian railways managed things better. During the days of the Raj, a train journey across the subcontinent could take a week. At each stop trains were besieged with hawkers selling everything from chapattis to a shave, but passengers could telegraph ahead so that a delicious and aromatic meal was brought on a tray covered with a napkin to the window of the carriage as the train drew into the next station. Were these platform luncheons and suppers the first Indian take-aways?

When Gladys Aylward, the unstoppable English missionary, set off for China from Liverpool Street Station in 1930, she had with her a suitcase containing hard-boiled eggs, meat cubes, tins of corned beef, baked beans, biscuits and soda cakes. These provisions were not barter for friendly natives but food for her mammoth journey across Europe, Russia, Siberia and Manchuria. She also had 9d, and a £2 Thomas Cook travellers cheque sewn into her corset. The story of this young woman's lone train journey across Europe and Asia is one of the most haunting of railway stories and powerfully told by Alan Burgess in his book *The Small Woman*. When the train stopped at the all-too-active battlefield in the frozen wastes of the Siberian-Manchurian border, her only hope was to walk back along the railway track to the previous station:

> She set off. Not many miles from the Manchurian border, the Siberian wind gusting the powdered snow round her heels, a suitcase in either hand, one still decorated ludicrously with kettle and saucepan, fur rug over her shoulders, she crunched off into the night. God obviously did not mean her to be eaten by the wolves, for there were plenty about.

Despite couchettes, electrification, high-speed trains, restaurant cars, and the arrival of the car and aeroplane, there are still travellers for whom rail journeys hold a particular magic, and places in the world where a journey by rail is almost as adventurous as Gladys Aylward's. The inveterate train traveller, Christopher Portway, who finds world train travel 'something of the elixir of life', warns that a journey by train through the Baluchistan Desert can be hazardous. The heat is so intense that the rails are likely to buckle and passengers are expected to help repair the track. If the rails are not bent they may be covered with

'Ten minutes for refreshment' 1892: passengers bolt their lunch at York station buffet prior to reboarding, in the days before buffet cars were provided.

In the days of the Raj, British passengers on the Rajputana State Railway received enviable attention: this handbook is a personalized itinerary for Miss Baring and warns her that she may be kept awake by one train driver's 'unpleasant whistle'.

Opposite Passengers crowd onto a train in India where the steam trains are legendary and still the dream of travellers.

drifting sand so that the train can only creep along, making it a perfect target for anti-government tribes who like to vent their political frustrations on the train. Portway claims that the slowest train in the world was one in which he travelled in Turkey. The driver, anxious to be the last word in customer care, drove at a snail's pace so that passengers could walk beside the train and pick flowers.

Railway lines criss-cross the globe from the lowest marshes to the mountain heights. There is a railway line in Peru which reaches 4,782 metres – the highest railway to carry passengers in the world. The air is so thin that when it reaches the highest point medical staff in white coats appear in the carriages to administer oxygen to passengers struck down by the altitude. Travel by train still holds the excitement and anticipation of a real journey. From a train the traveller sees the world pass by. Framed in the grimy windows is a

Grand Central station, New York.

The Lima to Huancayo train in Peru reversing up the next section of the highest railway in the world.

series of pictures rather like a personal film show: fleeting dramas of everyday life, and sometimes the astonishing beauty of an untouched landscape.

To help the traveller negotiate the world's railroads (about 800 thousand miles, 1.3 million kilometres of main routes) Thomas Cook publish two remarkable handbooks which together list the world's principal rail, shipping and bus timetables. The *Thomas Cook European Timetable* has been published since 1873 with a break only during the Second World War; *Thomas Cook Overseas Timetable* lists countries outside Europe and has been published since 1981. The *Overseas Timetable* is magical reading to the traveller, its tightly-packed pages tell the reader how to catch a train, bus or ship in about 8,300 places, from a frozen corner of Alaska to Zongo in Zaire. It even gives the colour of postboxes in Tonga, lists the Mississippi and the Amazon River boat services, and the romantic names of American trains: 'Night Owl', 'Silver Meteor', 'The Desert Wind', 'Silver Star', 'Broadway Ltd', 'Californian Zephyr', 'Sunset Ltd'. 'The Chatanooga Choo Choo' is there too. And with fine understatement it records where getting from A to B is virtually impossible: 'There are no rail services in Equatorial Guinea, few tarred roads, very few buses and no taxis.' But this traveller's bible also says that there are an awful lot of buses in Brazil.

Right The cover of *Cook's Continental Time Tables* first published in 1873. It later became the *Thomas Cook European Timetable*. *Below* The riverboat *Creole Queen* churns the waters of the Mississippi. *Bottom* The Union Pacific train 'Challenger Streamliner'. These trains cut twenty hours and thirty minutes off the running time of the 2299-mile journey between Chicago and Los Angeles when they came into service in 1954.

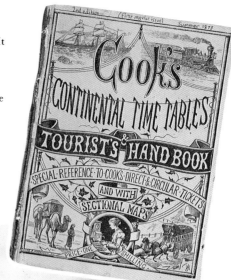

In remote parts of the world buses are often the only means of covering long distances.

Without the humble bus, travel in many parts of the world would be almost impossible. The traveller who rides on a local bus can learn a lot: in the mountains of Greece everyone clings on for dear life and makes the sign of the cross at every bend in the road; in the Thar Desert, Rajasthan, a sense of humour is essential, especially when the giggling driver moves the sheltering bus to reveal squatting passengers answering the call of nature, and in South America it helps if you don't mind sitting next to a chicken or sharing the floor with a goat. Even in affluent North America the bus is the only means of public transport between thousands of towns. Intercity buses in the United States carry 375 million passengers a year across more than a billion miles – quite a legacy from the first US bus service which operated on Long Island in 1899.

To the snobbish traveller coach tours are a subject of derision, but since the inter-war period when coach touring really took off, thousands of people who could not normally afford to travel have seen countries other than their own through the comparative cheapness of coach travel. In the early days the novelty must have outweighed the discomfort, or no one would have travelled in the first charabancs. They had no windows or windscreen and only a canopy and storm curtains for protection. The tyres were solid rubber and the seats hard. In Britain the legal speed limit was 12 mph but since they broke down frequently speed was of little consequence. Most excursions were local but standards improved rapidly and by 1924 there were coach tours from the UK to North Africa and by 1935 the charabanc had reached

The Greyhound bus goes to parts of America which other forms of transport cannot reach.

The People's car: hundreds of day-trippers brave the discomfort of a fleet of charabancs at Plymouth in 1922. *Inset below* Off on holiday: a family boards a coach in 1955. *Inset below right* Americans in London: Rodeo boys take a trip down Queen Victoria Street in June 1924.

Soviet Russia. By the 1950s some coaches had air-conditioning, lavatories, cocktail bars and kitchens.

Of course, the development of the internal combustion engine had a huge impact on travel. According to *Alliance Internationale de Tourisme* the private car now carries about 75 per cent of all

A procession of cars tours Glenshee, Scotland in 1923.

travellers. In Europe the craze for motoring took off in the twenties and thirties, helped in 1931 by the launching of the first cross-Channel ferry specifically designed to carry cars and their passengers.

Until the last century ships which only carried passengers were unknown. For centuries the traveller who wanted to cross a sea or an ocean went to the nearest port and hung about until he found a ship going in his direction. After that it was a matter of negotiating a passage with the captain and then waiting until the ship's cargo was loaded and the weather and omens were right for the voyage. This was still the practice by the 1830s when a tide of emigrants left Europe for Australia, New Zealand and California. But the number of emigrants forced the introduction of booking systems, although a booked passsage did not guarantee comfort. For many emigrants, conditions at sea were no better than for the animals these ships carried. Water came from a pump on deck and many families had to also cook their own meals on deck.

Distinguished guests fared only a little better '. . . a pleasant fiction and cheerful jest of the captain's . . . a profoundly preposterous box' was how Charles Dickens described his cabin on board the *Britannia* in which he crossed the Atlantic on his trip to America in 1842. Cramped cabins, often shared by several people and autocratic captains made life on board uncomfortable. On one ship passengers dared to open the windows of a saloon because it was rather stuffy. When the captain discovered this little act of initiative he changed course so that the sea roared in through the ports and flushed passengers and their game of cards from the room.

Seasickness was a problem. Sir Henry Bessemer suffered so badly that he designed an anti-seasick steamer whose saloon was supposed to stay on an even keel even if the ship rolled. It didn't work. As William Thackeray discovered on the world's first cruise aboard P & O ships in 1844, the Bay of Biscay sorts the good sailors from the bad:

> Before sunrise I had the good fortune to discover that it was no longer necessary to maintain the horizontal posture, and came out on deck at two o'clock in the morning to see a noble full moon sinking westward and millions of the most brilliant stars shining overhead.

Passengers and sailors had to wait until 1931 for a ship with stabilizers.

'I never saw such good use made of knives and forks before . . .' recorded a P & O passenger in his diary of a voyage east in the 1860s. Once stomachs had settled to life at sea their owners got down to the serious work of filling them with the gargantuan meals offered. After a bugle call to rise at 8.30 the day seemed to be spent eating: breakfast and lunch were followed by dinner at 4 p.m. which consisted of '. . . soup, various kinds of roasts, fowls etc., pastry, puddings . . . cheese and celery – dessert, consisting of apples, oranges, dried fruit etc.' All this was washed down with unlimited quantities of wine, beer, porter and champagne.

By 1918 there were very few sailing ships left on the major shipping routes. The first crossing of the Atlantic entirely under steam power was made in 1833 and the ships which travelled that route

Shipping lines continued to carry emigrants across the Atlantic during the twentieth century. This poster of 1906 lists opportunities for families, married couples, single people and boys. Under the Family Settlement Scheme the fare to Canada was £3.

Sir Henry Bessemer's anti-seasick steamer. The saloon was balanced on a central pivot. At sea it rolled so violently that passengers on upper decks were far less ill than those in the special saloon. She was eventually sold for scrap.

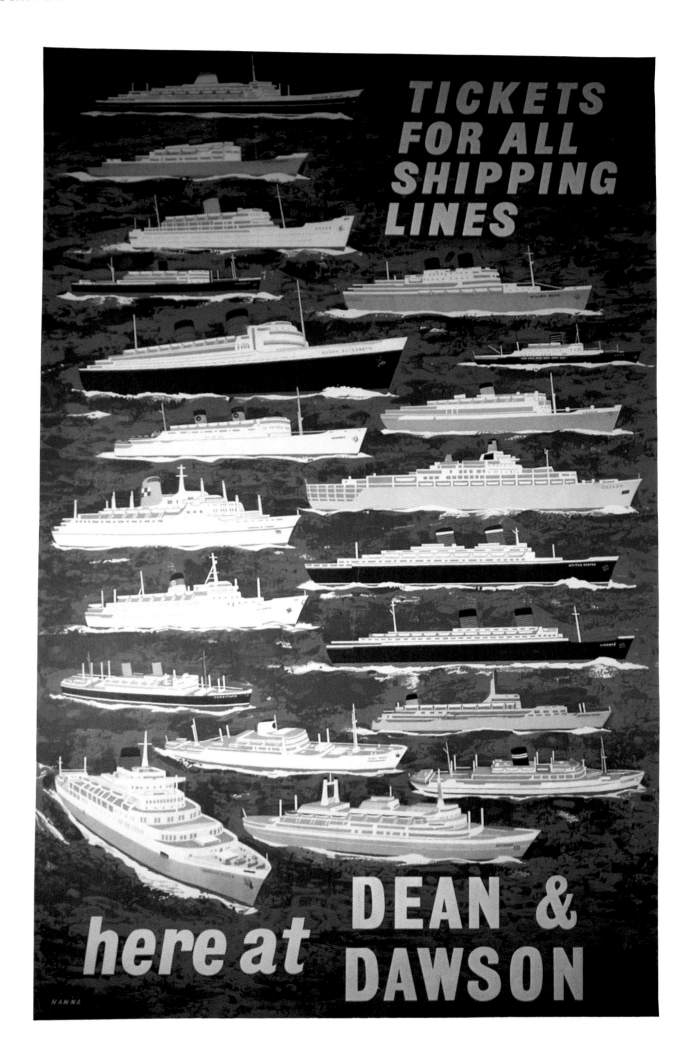

were among the most famous in the history of steamships: the *Mauretania* held the Blue Riband for the fastest Atlantic crossing, but after twenty-two years it was won by the *Queen Mary*. The majestic *Queens* began their Atlantic shuttle in the late 1940s carrying filmstars, tourists and businessmen across the chilly grey waters.

Passengers board the *Queen Mary* for her maiden voyage to Southampton in May 1936. *Inset* Cooks were agents for all the major shipping lines.

These great ships are now cruise liners and are the only passenger ships left which continue a stately form of travel where, as one enthusiast put it, 'there is nothing to do but be'. The reign of the ocean-going liners ended in 1958 when the first jet service crossed the Atlantic.

The plane flew so low that Freya Stark, aloft on her first flight in 1922, could see a fox running below. When the little aircraft bumped to a halt on a grassy field outside Paris, Miss Stark, who had chosen to travel in the outside cockpit for the sheer hell of it, put her hands to her head and tried to calm her dishevelled hair. She was lifted out of her perch above the engine and made for the customs shed where she asked for a mirror so that she could restore order to her wrecked coiffure before she went into Paris. The customs officers were very understanding and found a mirror and propped it up on the customs bench for her.

Opposite Shipping lines and their agents advertised throughout the nineteenth century and the first half of the twentieth century. This Dean and Dawson poster dates from the 1950s.

Passengers in the early days of air travel had to be courageous and long suffering – qualities still needed at some airports today. Facilities were very primitive; many passenger planes in 1919 were converted bombers, airports were fields with wooden huts for passenger terminals. If passengers chose to travel outside they were equipped with helmet and goggles. Sometimes the loan of a fur-lined flying suit was included in the price of the single ticket (London to Paris twenty guineas). Inside the aircraft passengers sat on wicker chairs, often surrounded by mail bags.

Pilots were expected to be jacks of all trades. If the cooling system sprang a leak pilots had to land and mend the pipe with chewing gum and insulation tape. Forced landings were common, even Charlie Chaplin was seen standing on the sands of Bologne in the early 1920s while his pilot fixed the aircraft. In Australia, pioneering QANTAS pilots often woke passengers in their hotel, cooked them breakfast, pushed the aircraft out of the hangar, loaded it with mail and freight and took off – all by the crack of dawn. They also had to clear up after passengers who were airsick.

The first regular, scheduled international service in the world began on 25 August 1919. The plane left London (Hounslow) for Paris (Le Bourget) with a mixed cargo of clotted cream, grouse, newspapers, a quantity of leather and some passengers. Deutsche Luft Reederei, the forerunner of Lufthansa, began in 1917 and the French also had a service in operation by 1919.

Holiday-makers in Blackpool in the summer of 1919 queued in their thousands for the thrill of taking a joy-ride over the famous sands. Ten thousand people were taken up for a guinea a ride of a few moments. Cooks did not miss the opportunity: that year they advertised half-hour trips in Handley Page aircraft which took off from Cricklewood, North London, and two thousand passengers flew on them. The joy-rides helped the public to overcome their fear of flying and these pleasure trips paved the way for scheduled commercial flights, which were first allowed later the same year. Cooks also published a far-sighted brochure in 1919 *Aerial Travel for Business or Pleasure* and by 1921 they were acting as agents for eighteen air companies.

All early air travellers and airlines had a pioneering spirit. When Imperial Airways was formed in 1924 to link the British Empire by a network of routes it had to overcome the problem of flying over featureless deserts with virtually no navigational aids. Their solution on the Egypt to India run was to get the RAF to plough a huge furrow across the desert which the pilots could follow. In those days planes could not fly vast distances and had to stop overnight, often in remote places. Imperial Airways built a fort for

The first flying cinema, 1925.

By air from Paris, 1922: passengers arriving in London are helped from the plane by their leather-coated pilot.

Holiday-makers struggle into an aircraft to take a joy-ride above Canvey Island, England, May 1923. Tea flights over London were also popular; tea and cakes were served in mid joy-ride, high above the city. *Inset above* Cooks guide to air travel, 1919. *Inset left* Cooks organized the first advertised chartered air tour in 1927, to view the world heavyweight champion Jack Dempsey defend his title against Gene Tunney. Dempsey lost.

passengers and planes in Persia to protect them from unwelcome visits by local tribesmen.

Chartering aircraft for pleasure began in the 1920s. In 1927, the year that Lindbergh flew solo across the Atlantic, Cooks chartered a plane to take fans from New York to Chicago to attend the Tunney-Dempsey boxing match. It was the first

Opposite A flying-boat takes off from Southampton Water.

Below The *Comet*, the first commercial jet airliner. It was inaugurated by BOAC on a flight from London to Johannesburg in May 1952. *Bottom* How one of the world's busiest airports began life. Passenger terminals and communications, London's Heathrow, 1946.

advertised air tour and the price included a ringside seat and hotel accommodation. In 1931 the Polytechnic Touring Association organized the first air charter holiday, flying twenty-four passengers from Croydon, south of London, in a four-engined Heracles.

A leader comment in the *Observer* newspaper of 1934 acknowledged that a revolution in travel was underway:

> The air must be the highway of the future for all who would live greatly – whether individuals or communities . . . to be behind on the aerial road will spell secondrateness in everything.

In 1939 PAN AM launched the first transatlantic airline service on *Yankee Clipper*, a Boeing 314 flying boat with all mod cons – even

sleeping berths and a bridal suite. But the war stopped progress and the world had to wait until the 1950s for the next major innovations in civilian flight.

The *Comet*, brought into service in 1952, was the first commercial jet and although design faults made its supremacy short, it paved the way for faster and faster travel. The 1960s saw the proliferation of charter flights and the 1970s brought mass travel with the 747s – the 'Jumbo' jets. Supersonic passenger flights on *Concorde* began in 1976. Tens of millions of passengers pass through busy airports like London's Heathrow every year, which can sometimes make travellers furious, but not very fast. It is a long flight from the early days when pilots taking off from Cricklewood in North London looked out of the cockpit and saw the number sixteen bus overtaking them.

Early air travellers often flew for adventure, not just speed, and some travellers today, who do not have to cram a two-week break into a busy year, have gone back to earlier forms of transport which give them a far sharper sense of going places. Cyclists get everywhere. Nick Crane, a Fellow of the Royal Geographical Society, has ridden his bike to the world's furthest point from the sea, a spot in the Gobi Desert which he reached after cycling across the Himalayas and the Tibetan Plateau. Dervla Murphy has cycled from her home in Ireland to India and many places in between, and Bettina Selby has pedalled from the mouth to the source of the Nile. These contemporary cyclists are part of a grand tradition of bicycling travellers. The penny farthing was an extremely difficult bicycle to ride, but Thomas Stevens left San Francisco on one in 1884 and returned two years later having ridden 13,500 miles round the world. John Foster Fraser and two friends cycled round the world on more conventional cycles in 1896, but 19,237 miles must have felt very tough on the slow, heavy bikes of the time. Motorcyclists have also tackled round-the-world journeys. Paul Pratt travelled through forty-eight countries. It took him thirteen years and he covered over a hundred thousand miles. Afterwards he wrote a book about his experiences, *World Understanding on Two Wheels*.

Travel on two or four legs is the most ancient way of getting around the world. Thomas Coryate wrote that he covered 'a verie immense dimension of ground' when he walked to India and back to England in 1612. How many people today would be able to walk six thousand miles? But of the remaining remote and unspoilt places left on earth many can only be reached on foot, or with the help of pack animals.

'Camels go on and on and on until they die; and then one has the option of eating them,

The penny farthing made its first appearance in 1870 and was ridden round the world in 1884.

Some travellers still prefer muscle power: cycling in India.

altogether far better tasting than a Michelin tyre,'
writes René Dee in *The Traveller's Handbook*. After
most people's experiences of travelling on camels
they would probably find a penny farthing easier,
but Robyn Davidson trekked 1,700 miles across
the Australian desert with two camels and a dog
for company. Robert Louis Stevenson, the novelist

Travelling with yaks in the Himalayas.

and poet who travelled extensively, preferred the
donkey. In 1878 he tramped through the Cevennes
with a donkey named Modestine and discovered
the delights of *Travels with a Donkey*. Travelling
with yaks needs a certain kind of nerve as they
can be mean and quarrelsome animals: perhaps
that is why Peter Somerville-Large named the two
hairy four-foots who allowed him to travel with
them through Nepal and Tibet, Mucker and Sod.

Although there are now trains which can travel
in excess of 200 mph, supersonic planes which
take passengers across the Atlantic in three hours,
and spacecraft which can carry passengers at
fifteen times the speed of sound, our ancestors
used more stylish forms of transport. Lord
Auckland, Governor General of India in the 1830s,
left Calcutta to tour the Upper Provinces in 1837
with an entourage of twelve thousand people,
140 elephants, hundreds of horses and bullocks
and 850 camels. His transport manager must have
had nightmares finding parking places for a
caravan of that size. But it seems that whatever
the century or means of transport, parking is
always a problem: in the seventh century BC
Sennacharib, King of Assyria, decreed that anyone
who parked a chariot on the processional way to
his capital would be punished by impaling.

Overleaf The bullet train speeds past Mount Fuji.

CHAPTER *5*

Travelling in Style

SOME WAYS OF TRAVELLING are synonymous with luxury and romance and evoke nostalgic yearnings for the great days of travel when black tie was *de rigueur* as the traveller sauntered through Europe and Asia, or crossed the oceans. One of the most romantic ways of travelling was aboard the great floating palaces, the transatlantic liners, as they sped across the Atlantic to and from New York in the 1920s and '30s. As the sound of the siren resonated across New York harbour, passengers left their hotels and made their way by taxi to the piers where ship after ship (there were at least ten crossings a week to Europe in the summer of 1929) nosed the city's waterfront. The razzmatazz on the quay heralded the style of the crossing. Taxis, limousines and chauffeur-driven Rolls Royces disgorged their occupants and luggage – twenty trunks or more for some passengers – into a crowd of porters, stewards, sleek businessmen, tycoons, bright young things, would-be débutantes, aristocrats, parvenus, celebrities, movie-stars, and all the families and friends who made up the send-off party. Bands played, there were minute by minute deliveries of orchids and gardenias and the miniature lightning of flashlights lit the crowd as photographers dived among the luminaries.

Once embarkation was complete, the great ship slipped her moorings and slid out into the Atlantic garlanded with thousands of waving hands and handkerchiefs, blown kisses and streamers. Tiny vessels fussed in her wake like pilot fish around a whale and aircraft roared past her portholes. On board, the passengers explored. They had six days to do absolutely nothing in luxurious surroundings.

Great cruise liners, including the *Normandie*, the *Britannic* and the *Aquitania* (fifth, sixth and seventh from bottom), on New York's waterfront, 1939.

Opposite Still glamorous, New York harbour today.

Left Hundreds of paper streamers herald the departure of the *Empress of Scotland*, 1925. *Below* The *Normandie*, one of the most opulent liners, steams from Le Havre, watched by thousands on the quayside.

No other shipping company had quite the
cachet of Cunard and its ships were among the
most opulent that cut the Atlantic waves. The
Aquitania's 3,230 passengers could take a dip in a
swimming pool decorated with Egyptian motifs
and surrounded by columns, or enjoy an after-
dinner cigarette in the seventeenth-century

Left The grandeur of the
colonnaded bathing pool on
board the White Star liner
Majestic, 1934. *Below* The
Majestic's Palm Court lived
up to her name.

Carolean smoking room. The ceiling of the
Palladian lounge was sumptuously painted with
classical themes framed in gilded plasterwork. The
seven hundred diners in the Louis XVI restaurant
sat on elegant *petit point* chairs surrounded by
delicate columns and banks of flowers, and chose
from over eighty dishes on the menu: oysters,
lobster, caviare, game, beef, tongue, soufflés,
profiteroles and *petits fours* – and the champagne
flowed.

Other ships were no less extravagant: the
French Line's *Île de France* whose passenger list
was positively electric with names: Marlene
Dietrich, Toscanini, Cecil B. de Mille, Gloria
Swanson and John D. Rockefeller, was adorned
with sculptures and paintings, Lalique glass light
fittings, Pyrenean marble and sweeping movie-
star staircases. The *Normandie's* dining salon was
described as 'a tour de force of tinted glass . . .
longer than the famed Hall of Mirrors at
Versailles. . . . The huge main doors were gilt over
bronze and led out to a stairway that swept up to
an entrance vestibule lined with Algerian onyx.' In
such opulent surroundings the journey itself
became a luxurious holiday.

Most ships catered for every need. There were music rooms, hairdressing salons, beauty parlours, libraries, laundries, chapels, theatres, ballrooms, nurseries, and gymnasiums and health clubs armed with equipment which by modern standards appear more intent on medieval torture than health improvement. By day passengers played deck games, indulged in a little light conversation in conservatory-style cafés complete with potted palms and rattan furniture, or promenaded the decks dressed in the fashion essentials of plus-fours and Chanel sweaters or pyjamas de bâteau. By night the mood changed, there was dining, dancing and gambling. Out came the jewels and bare shoulders, the silk georgette and gold tissue. The passengers may have been ablaze with diamonds, but the ships themselves were lit at every porthole and festooned with lights, as they moved relentlessly through the dark Atlantic waters like brilliant spaceships intent on terrestrial encounters.

Encounters of the romantic kind were frequent on ocean liners. In his guidebook, *The Frantic Atlantic*, published in 1927, Basil Woon strongly advised that the dinner jacket was vital to a gentleman's chances. 'Without it you will have no dances and no Great Moments with the young thing in crepe-marocain on the lee of the starboard ventilator.' Such moments were not confined to Atlantic crossings. 'It' was all happening at sea. As *Vogue* stated in a 1920 cruise report, 'The Master-At-Arms' stern duty is to drive late lovers out of the lifeboats.' In Charles Allen's book, *Plain Tales From The Raj* a colonial traveller describes how romance could cut across the great social divide – almost. A governor's daughter, travelling to India, found the first-class passengers stuffy and took a fancy to a handsome second-class steward with whom she danced at the fancy dress ball. They parted at dawn but when he approached her later the same morning she froze him with an icy gaze and said, 'In the circle in which I move, sleeping with a man does not constitute an introduction.' The frailties of the holiday romance have a long history.

Rich and titled passengers often travelled with several servants including a lady's maid, butler, valet, nursery maid, footman and nanny. The valet and lady's maid sometimes travelled first class to be on hand for their employer's needs. The staffing of the liners was lavish too. The ratio of service staff to passengers was frequently about one to three, and that did not include seamen. The *Queen Mary* carried 1,995 passengers and 1,285 crew. Among the staff were chefs, kitchen staff, head waiters, waiters, barmen, stewards and stewardesses, a doctor, nurses, hairdressers, barbers, musicians, florists, laundry-workers, starchers and ironers, tailor's pressers and wardrobe-keepers.

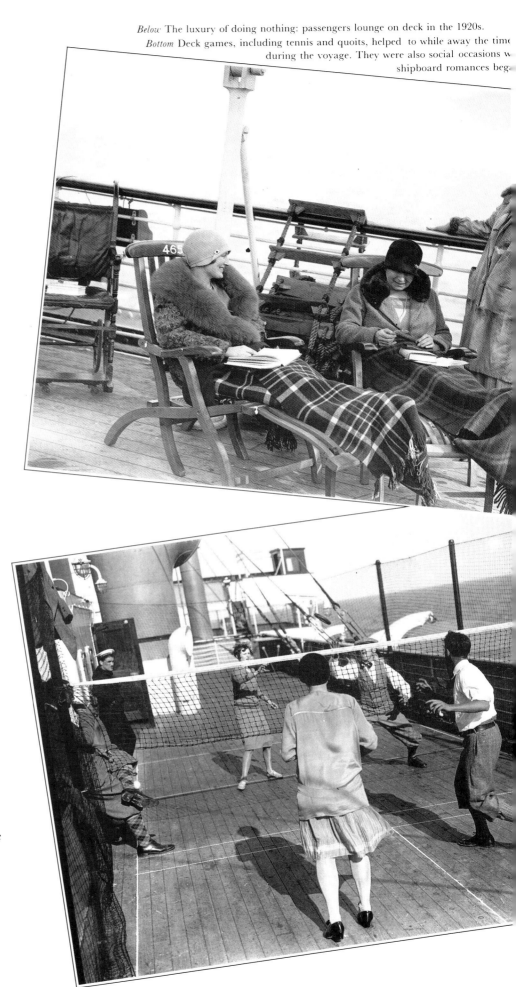

Below The luxury of doing nothing: passengers lounge on deck in the 1920s.
Bottom Deck games, including tennis and quoits, helped to while away the time during the voyage. They were also social occasions w[...] shipboard romances beg[...]

Clockwise Young lovers took to the lifeboats, not to save their souls but to pursue their
romance in private; passenger comforts included beauty salons: a 'young thing'
takes a Turkish bath on the *Berengaria*, 1923; tiny tots also tasted luxury
aboard: a menu for a children's tea party, 1933; as this menu
from the *Normandie* shows, the cuisine on board
these liners was a gourmet's delight.

The number of staff devoted to the care of clothes reflects the importance of a traveller's wardrobe. The magazines of the time carried article after article laying down the law of correct and essential dress in which to be seen on ocean crossings and cruises. *Vogue* recommended comfortable sports clothes and the obligatory pyjamas de bâteau for day wear. At tea-time it was essential to change into something 'sleek, black and Parisian'. After that it was time to change for dinner – to shine but not to shriek. In her bible of etiquette, published in 1922, Emily Post scathingly dismissed women who dressed in ballgowns:

> [it] is in the worst possible taste, and, like overdressing in public places, indicates that they have no other place to show their finery. People of position never put on formal evening dress on a steamer . . .

Anyone who did not read Miss Post's book before their first voyage had only themselves to blame for sartorial gaffes. In that era, so much of the day was spent climbing in and out of the correct clothes that there can't have been much time left for recreation. It is said that when travelling by boat the Duchess of Windsor sent to the bridge for hourly weather reports to be sure that she was appropriately clad.

Vogue lists the traveller's wardrobe for voyages and destinations in detail. In the 1920s the magazine advised that gloves are not worn much in India and four pairs, at least two of which should be evening gloves, will do. Pair after pair of shoes are needed too:

> . . . at least one pair of walking shoes to wear with tweeds, another to wear with washing frocks, a smart pair of shoes for afternoon, several pairs of sandals for morning, several pairs to go with evening dresses, bedroom slippers and shoes for sports.

And then there were hats for every occasion, sunglasses, sportswear and even the questionable piece of advice that a firm corset would prevent seasickness. It is no wonder that many passengers arrived on board with dozens of pieces of luggage and that the periodicals were full of adverts for trunks with unbelievable numbers of drawers, compartments, locks, straps, flaps and buckles. 'Travelling light' was clearly not a phrase known to the pampered passengers aboard the magnificent *Queens* of the seas. But all that had to change when the smart set took to the air.

When Lady Maud Hoare flew from Britain to India in 1926 on the first ever flight from Croydon to Delhi she had to reduce the amount of luggage

No stylish female passenger cruised across the Atlantic without pyjamas de bâteau, essential dress for lounging on deck. *Inset* The right travelling bags denoted the smart set, some of whom came with dozens of pieces of luggage and servants to unpack them.

with which she usually travelled quite drastically.
It wasn't easy; as wife of the British Air Minister
she had many official engagements to attend
en route and needed a suitable wardrobe. She
managed to pare it down to two skirts, two
jumpers, a cardigan, three coats, a hat, a dressing
gown and a black lace evening dress. She also
included a pair of gum boots which she found
'most useful on wet aerodromes'. The leather
baggage and glass cosmetic pots of the day were
too heavy to take on the plane but she managed to
find lighter substitutes and so became a pioneer of
lightweight luggage, as well as a pioneer female
passenger.

'As surely as the woman of yesterday was born
to ride in a limousine, the woman of today was
born to ride in an aeroplane' pronounced *Vogue* in
the 1920s. Flying was thrilling and romantic and
taking to the air was for women of spirit while
those who stayed on the ground had feet of clay.
Early female aviators were not short on glamour
either. When Sophie Heath flew solo from the
Cape to Cairo in 1928, the first woman to make
the trip, she managed to wriggle out of her flying
suit just before touchdown, and don an outfit in
which to make an entrance. She emerged
triumphantly from her plane wearing dress, coat,
hat, pearls and silk stockings.

Early passenger planes were not comfortable but
from about 1928 through the 1930s standards
improved to give facilities which today's
passengers would envy. On planes such as
Luft Hansa's *Junkers G31* seating was arranged like
a first-class railway carriage and meals were taken
at little tables for two spread with pristine linen,
full silver and fresh flowers. Food and drink were
extremely important and luncheon might consist
of pâté de foie gras, lobster, roast chicken and
York ham with all the trimmings followed by
pêche Melba, cheese and biscuits, crystallized
fruits, coffee and liqueurs, washed down with fine
wines and vast quantities of champagne. This was
travelling in style – as one Imperial Airways
passenger put it: 'I was sorry to get out; it had
been like sitting in a comfortable friendly club.'
And, of course, it was still possible to open the
windows. . . .

On long routes there were many overnight stops
when passengers were put up in luxury hotels and
enjoyed a night on the town. In those days
Imperial Airlines staff were expected to know the
local '. . . going rate for a lady of pleasure, and at
what time the night clubs closed and what was the
price of a gin and tonic.' As planes improved they
could fly further between stops and passengers
slept on board. By comparison with trying to sleep
on the cramped seating of today's long-haul flights
it was luxury indeed. Passengers actually changed
into their pyjamas and settled down for the night

Tucked up for the night on a long-haul flight.

The airlines of today would find it difficult to compete with the
luxury of meal service on Luft Hansa in 1928. The cabin
arrangement followed the style of first class rail travel.

in bunks or convertible seat-beds complete with
sheets and blankets. In the morning they
experienced the delight of tea in bed cruising
above the clouds.

Such cosseting made passengers feel they were
very special and the airlines did all they could to
encourage distinguished people to fly with them.

Imperial Airways carried HM King Feisal from
Baghdad to Gaza in 1927 and later took to
publishing monthly lists of their important
passengers. In March 1932 the list included Lord
Londonderry, Secretary of State for Air, Baron
Rothschild, Prince and Princess Walkonsky, two
racing drivers, a French film producer and an MP.
Releasing the list to the press sometimes
backfired: on one occasion a wife read in a
newspaper that she and her husband had flown to
Paris for the weekend. It was news to her, she had
been at home all the time and her husband had
taken another 'wife'. Imperial Airways had
difficulty in extricating themselves from the
ensuing row. By 1935 passenger lists were as
glittering as those of the ocean liners; insurance
companies had decided that aeroplanes were safe
for their valuable clients and many Hollywood
actors and actresses took to the skies like the stars
they were.

Glamour aloft was also provided by the great
airships *Graf Zeppelin* and *Hindenburg*. *Graf Zeppelin*

The great airship *Graf Zeppelin* cruises away from her moorings.
She made a round-the-world trip in 1929.

made its first flight in 1928, the *Hindenburg* in 1936. Both were sumptuously decorated but the *Hindenburg* was the most luxurious. In addition to twenty-five cabins it had three bars, a dining room which measured fifteen by fifty feet, a lounge with a baby grand piano, a writing room, library and sick bay. There was also a smoking room where a

Opposite Poster for an exhibition to celebrate the glories of the *Zeppelins*. One of their main attractions were the promenade decks from which passengers could look down on seas, rivers, forests and cities.

steward was in constant attendance to light pipes and cigars; he was the only person on board permitted to use matches.

The *Zeppelins*' glory was short-lived and ended in well-documented disaster, but in the 1930s the most romantic of all planes, the flying-boat, came to the fore. The name *Empire Flying-boat* rings with nostalgia and is linked forever with exotic destinations, superb food, attentive service and surfing to a halt on one of Africa's great lakes or the brilliant waters of a tropical sea. The Americans also developed the flying-boat. Those belonging to Pan American were called *Clippers*; they flew the Pacific and the Atlantic and, when storms were violent, they flew so low that the spray from the waves broke over the aircraft. By the last of the series these flying-boats with their deluxe suites and dining salons had reached the height of spaciousness and comfort. No plane like it has since been used by the public.

In 1942 Cecil Beaton returned to England in a flying-boat from a three month tour of Egypt, Iraq and Persia as an official war photographer. After take-off Beaton surveyed his surroundings; 'Silk-lined walls, arm chairs like Pullmans, various compartments for eating, sleeping, smoking – this is the aircraft that took Churchill to America . . . how grateful I am to be among the lucky ones on the last lap for home.' The last flying-boat service out of Britain was in 1958. After that the solid throb of their engines and the thrill of seeing them skim to a halt on the waters of Poole Harbour were mere memories, although they continued to give excellent service in other parts of the world

Top Flying-boats had a glamorous image, but disembarking was often an undignified scramble. *Above* Pioneer woman passenger Lady Maude Hoare, her husband (then British Secretary of State for Air) and son watch a *Blackburn 'Iris' Flying-boat* skimming the waves in about 1925.

and a travel company has recently introduced a nostalgic flying-boat holiday across Africa on the route once used by Imperial Airways.

But a journey by steam train evokes more nostalgia and romance than any other way of travelling. The haunting sound of the whistle echoing through mountains at night, the

Opposite Steam locomotives are synonymous with the romance of travel: the 'Flying Scotsman' pulls out of King's Cross station, London, on a journey north in 1932.

thundering plunge across the plains, the astonishing restraint of such powerful giants as they inch in and out of stations have made them the inspiration of poets, writers, composers and film makers. Once on board and moving, the excited anticipation of the platform left behind, the traveller is held in a trance of observation as the world passes by. You see so much from a train. What else gives such a sense of covering the miles, of ground passing beneath the wheels, of travelling? The train newly arrived on a European platform may be covered in dust blown from the Gobi Desert, or encrusted with salt spray from the Bosporus.

It was in order to reach the Bosporus in style and comfort that Georges Nagelmackers created the 'Orient Express' which first steamed out of the Gare de l'Est in Paris in 1883, its passengers bound for Constantinople. What opulence they met as they settled into their private salons: Spanish leather armchairs embossed with gold, mahogany panelling inlaid with rosewood marquetry, damask curtains held by silk cords with gold tassels, thickly-carpeted floors, and each compartment was heated. At night they were lit by chandeliers and when the seats were converted to beds they were covered in silk sheets and fine woollen blankets. Along the corridor the toilet cabinet was full of Italian marble, decorated porcelain, fresh towels, soap and vials of toilet water. Few deluxe hotels of the time offered such luxury.

Top left The waiting room of Nyugati station, in Budapest, built like a palace to receive passengers from the 'Orient Express'. *Above* A poster advertises this most romantic of all trains. It made its first journey in 1883 but by the 1960s had been run down to an ordinary train. From 1977 the original coaches were found and restored to magnificence and the 'Orient Express' was relaunched as a luxury train in 1982.

Top Passengers board, bound for
Venice. *Above* Wagon-lit luxury.
Right Toilet cabinet on the
'Orient Express'.

Right Comfort and style on board
the luxurious 'Orient Express'.
Below Decorative panels of
Lalique glass. *Bottom* The
'Orient Express' travelling
through Alpine scenery.

The train was a triumph. It had a smoking-room
with fitments and atmosphere to rival the most
exclusive gentleman's club, a ladies' drawing-room
like a miniature boudoir with silk, tapestry and
chaise-longue in the style of Louis XV, but the *pièce
de résistance* was the dining-car. Here passengers
ate delicacies prepared by a master chef under an

'Orient Express' staff in 1930s-style livery.

arched ceiling of embossed leather and oil
paintings. The walls were exquisitely panelled and
bordered with carved scrolls and cornices
decorated with gilded flowers. There was an
abundance of Gobelins tapestries and Gênes
velvet. The table settings would not have
disgraced a banquet: fine Baccarat crystal, gold-
crested porcelain and solid silver cutlery set on
damask cloths. The waiters were dressed in velvet
knee breeches, silk stockings and tail coats, their
heads topped with powdered wigs (although these
were later discarded because, it is said, a
passenger complained that powder had dropped
into his soup).

No wonder the train eventually became the
focus of bandits, thieves and pickpockets. Its
passengers were as rich as its decor – diplomats,
royalty, aristocrats, tycoons, actors and opera
singers were its frequent patrons over the decades.
Even accompanying pets were lavishly treated.
A Hapsburg Archduchess, travelling to take her
four poodles for a Parisian clipping, had them fed

Dining car on the 'Orient Express' today.

three times a day on milk calf fried in Normandy butter. The fare of each dog almost equalled that of a human passenger.

The history of the 'Orient Express' is laced with romance. Smugglers, drug addicts and couriers were frequent travellers, and if all the stories are to be believed the train carried every spy from the notorious Mata Hari to the faceless agents of the Cold War. Today it is more likely to carry honeymooning couples to Venice, but it still retains a reputation as the ultimate in stylish travel.

There were and are other trains whose very names conjure excitement, among them: 'Train Bleu', 'Golden Arrow', 'Sud', 'Bombay Express', 'Raj Express', 'Al Andalus Expreso' and the 'Trans-Siberian International Express', also built by M. Nagelmackers, which had a gymnasium, library, music room, hairdressing salon and an entire wagon constructed as a chapel. But it was an American whose vision prompted such grand travel.

The vast distances covered by American railways meant that passengers often had to sleep on trains, but sleepers on early American trains were uncomfortable. George Mortimer Pullman, woodworker and lover of beautiful things, transformed American travel by train, and subsequently train travel worldwide, by creating the Pullman car in the 1860s. Polished wood, carpets, silvery oil lamps, upholstered seats and gilt-edged mirrors made Pullman's railway carriages into Victorian drawing-rooms on wheels by day and luxurious sleeping cars by night. 'Never before', wrote Joseph Husband, 'had such a car been seen; never had the wildest flights of fancy imagined such magnificence.'

It was the forerunner of every luxurious railway carriage, of which the private American railroad car, popular with tycoons between 1890 and the Second World War, was the ultimate status symbol of the traveller. These emblems of material success, most of which were built by Pullman, were coupled to regular trains to convey their owners across America. On such journeys men of means and their families wanted for nothing. Apart from the extravagance of the decor, there were food stores which could take a complete stag, racks for carrying vulgar quantities of champagne, sunken bathtubs, jewel safes, and gold dinner services. A certain Mrs E.T. Stotesbury ordered gold-plated plumbing in her car on the grounds that it would 'save so much polishing, you know'. Cissy Patterson, publisher of the Washington *Times-Herald*, had fresh flowers brought aboard at stopping places along the way. One son of a senator lived in hope: the partition wall separating his double bed from the one in the guest suite next door could be removed at the pull of a lever.

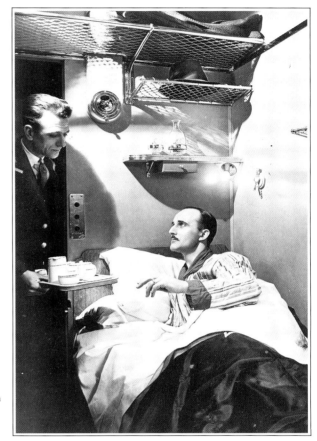

Early morning tea as a train plunges across Europe.

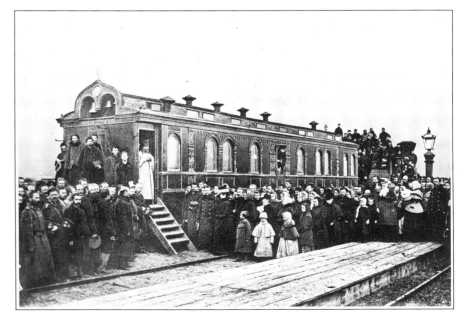

A service on the travelling chapel of the Trans-Siberian Express, 1906.

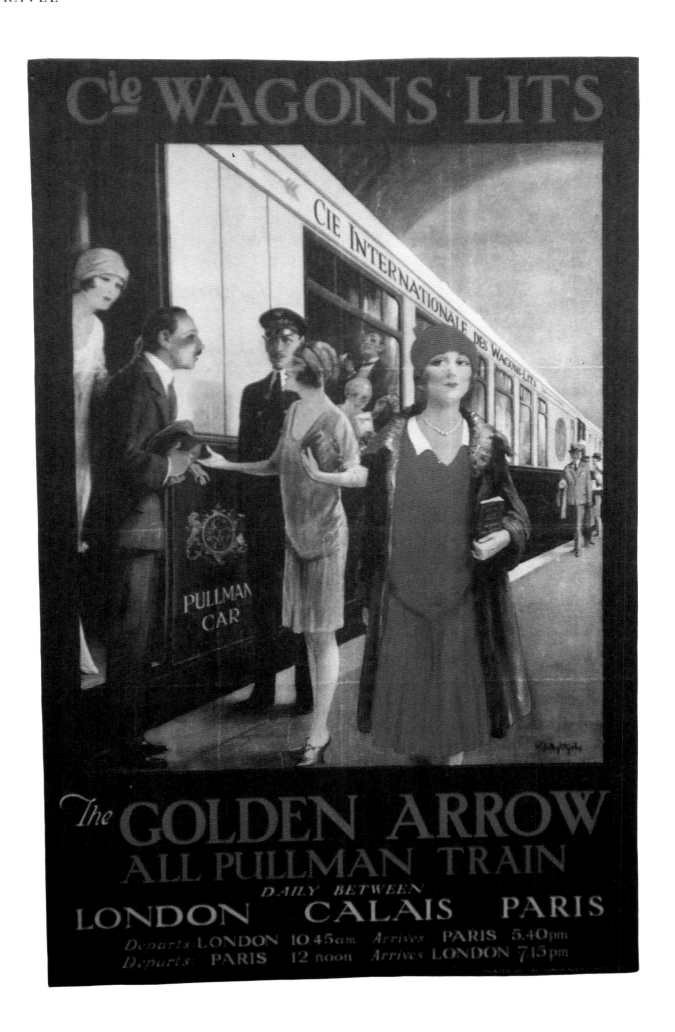

Such personalized luxury is still available only to the gargantuanly rich who have their own yachts and jets in which to make journeys. Most of us travel long distances by schedule or charter flights, cramped together in ranks of seats where there isn't enough room to stretch out the shortest leg, let alone walk about as passengers on the

Opposite The 'Golden Arrow' began its London-to-Paris run in 1926.

Flying in style today is epitomized in the powerful elegance of *Concorde. Inset* Watching the world go by from the observation or promenade deck of an *Empire Flying-boat*, 1930s.

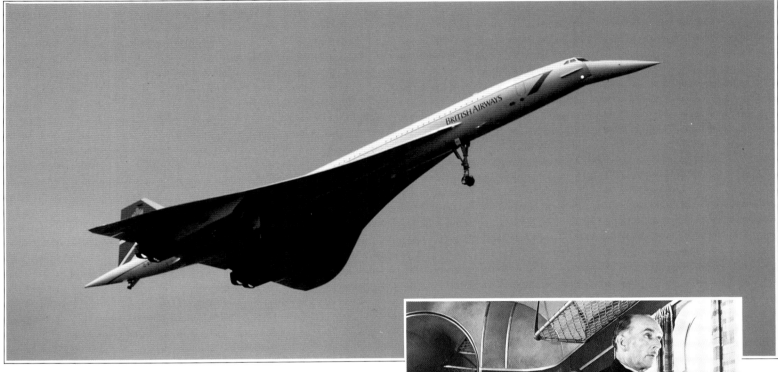

Empire Flying-boat or *Zeppelin* observation platforms could. But more people today can have a taste of travel and experience its intrinsic glamour than was possible fifty years ago, when only the well-off and aristocrats could afford to spend the time and money going abroad.

In the past people regarded the journey between two places as important and felt that it should be achieved with as much style and enjoyment as possible. Today the journey is, for most people, secondary to the destination. Young people with backpacks and habitual travellers may know what it means to go on a journey, but for most the romance of escape begins with deciding where to go on holiday and then getting there as quickly as possible.

If nostalgia for another age is high on the list then there are hotels of special quality and character which still offer the sort of service and ambience which were the hallmark of the grand days of travel. Their names exude glamour: the Cipriani, Venice; Raffles, Singapore; the Ritz, Paris; the Taj Mahal, Bombay; the Algonquin, New York; the Pera Palas, Istanbul; Sacher, Vienna; and the Dorchester, London. There are others, but these appear on many travellers' lists of favourite hotels.

Overleaf Set between the mountains and Lake Louise: the exclusive Canadian Pacific Hotel in the Rockies.

As the holiday-maker travels further and learns
more of the possibilities the world has to offer
through travel books, magazines and television,
travel companies are creating more and more
imaginative and flexible packages. It has been
possible for some time to cruise down the Nile, or
stay in some of the jewelled and painted palaces
of Moghul India, or walk along the Great Wall of
China. Now there are organized trips to Antarctica
for the experience and the wildlife; to the remotest

of Pacific islands sailing in a tall ship; to cross
Africa by flying-boat or hot-air balloon, or to
travel through the Arabian Desert by camel in the
steps of Lawrence of Arabia. And if you really
want to get away from it all you can hire a whole
Caribbean island, all to yourself.

It is even possible to take on the world.

Cooks have organized round-the-world tours since 1872.

To celebrate Thomas Cook's 150th anniversary
(1841–1991) the company organized a round-the-
world tour, just as the 'Grand Courier Extraordinary
to the Human Race' himself had in 1872. Thomas
Cook's original journey was the first organized
world tour. He travelled with his party and the
journey took eight months visiting America, Japan,
Hong Kong, China, India, Egypt, Palestine,
Turkey, and so homeward across Europe. 'This
going round the world is a very easy and almost
imperceptible business; there is no difficulty about
it', he wrote to *The Times* from a ship in the middle
of the Pacific in November 1872. What would the
grand old man of travel have made of the thirty-
nine days scheduled for the 1991 world tour?
Being such a shrewd organizer he would probably
have been delighted at the speed.

Opposite A spectacular way to see wildlife: a hot air balloon drifts
across the Masai Mara in Kenya. *Inset* The perfect desert island:
Kuda Bandos Island in the Maldives.

CHAPTER 6

The World Business

TRAVEL IS BIG BUSINESS. It is one of the world's fastest growing industries and if it maintains its present rate of growth it will be the world's biggest industry by the year 2000 – larger even than the oil industry. One hundred and fifty years ago it did not exist, but at the opening of the present decade the UK alone claimed to generate a thousand new jobs a week in the travel and tourism sector. In 1989, at least 300 million international journeys were made outbound from the major developed countries alone. As Miles Quest, writer on and consultant to the tourist industry, said in 1990, '. . . armies of people are on the move, and will not stop'.

More people are travelling than ever before and a complex and thriving industry has grown up to enable people to move round the world with comparative ease and speed. Before the industrial revolution of the early nineteenth century people travelled mainly for two reasons: either for business, or to go on a pilgrimage. There were a privileged few who made the Grand Tour to complete their education and seek out Europe's art treasures, but travelling for pleasure was not an accepted part of life as it is in Western industrialized countries today. Thomas Cook changed all that and practically invented the tourist industry single-handed, although his first efforts were often financially unrewarding and he kept his 'day' job as a printer. His belief in travel for the common man was so strong that he overcame many financial difficulties to establish his business.

Thomas Cook began as a tour operator organizing and selling his own tours and soon became an agent as well, selling all kinds of travel

The Phoenicians were successful business travellers; trading throughout the eastern Mediterranean and beyond, they travelled extensively.

Opposite Japanese business centre in Shinjuku, Tokyo.

on behalf of other suppliers, particularly the railway companies.

Cook rationalized and simplified travel arrangements with his innovations. In the 1860s he introduced the circular ticket which gave the traveller a single ticket to cover a journey rather than a handful from all the separate railway companies involved. In 1867 he introduced hotel coupons which were exchanged for meals and accommodation at hotels with whom Cook had arrangements. Hotel coupons paved the way for package holidays because tourists paid for facilities in advance in their own currency, in their own country instead of hunting for somewhere to stay and paying hotel bills as they went. It was a successful scheme, popular with travellers and with hoteliers who clamoured to get their hotels on to the prestigious Cook's list.

For many travellers, money was a problem. Carrying large quantities of cash was dangerous and inconvenient, and trying to secure cash on a letter of credit could be extremely difficult. In New York in 1874 Cook launched a system which made money available abroad against money deposited at home. He called this early form of travellers cheque a 'circular note'. The circular note could be cashed at hotels with which Cook had arrangements and a limited number of banks and bureaux de change. By 1880 there were about a thousand hotels in the scheme which proved a resounding success. Cook was not the first to put the idea into practice however; circular notes were first seen in an organized system invented by Robert Herries in 1772. Herries's circular notes were negotiable in about ninety cities across Europe and even in Moscow, and were still in use in 1839.

There has long been controversy over who invented the travellers cheque. Cook's circular note was its forerunner but Marcellus Berry patented the name 'Travelers Cheque' for American Express much later in 1891. As we enter the 1990s American Express and Thomas Cook are still the world's largest issuers of travellers cheques, and many savings institutions, travel agents and banks have followed their example, making the travellers cheque readily available.

Cooks organized travel included excursions to important sporting events.

Right and below Thomas Cook's revolutionary hotel coupons and circular ticket simplified travel and introduced the concept of package holidays. *Bottom* Travellers cheques freed travellers from the worry of carrying or transferring large sums of money. The original American Express 'travelers cheque'; guaranteed against loss or theft. *Bottom centre* Cook's circular note, forerunner of the travellers cheque. *Bottom left* Cook's travellers cheque.

Travel agents are now a familiar sight in towns and cities across the world but one hundred and fifty years ago there were very few. Most travellers had to make their own arrangements with coach, railway or shipping companies. Thomas Cook set up his London office in Fleet Street in 1865. The top floors of the building were converted into an hotel owned by Cook and run by his wife Marianne. Their son John Mason was in charge of the office on the ground floor. To keep it solvent in the early days the office sold travel goods such as baggage, guidebooks and walking-sticks in addition to the tours and other travel arrangements, which were the main source of

income. Recently, travel industry experts forecast that during the 1990s specialist travel shops will open where customers will be able to buy travel goods and equipment alongside their tickets and package holidays – Cook was always in the forefront of business ideas.

By 1877 Cook was successful enough to appoint sub-agents in several towns in northern England who sold their tours at 2½ per cent commission.

Thomas Cook's Fleet Street office decked with garlands for the coronation of King George V, 22 June 1911. *Inset* A window display advertising Cook's many services. Note the Nile poster and the model of the *Empire Flying-boat*.

Opposite Satisfying the customer: a nineteenth-century Cook's office.

Travel wholesaling is common practice today but Cooks pioneered it so successfully that they were issuing printed standard contracts to their agents by 1884. The idea really took off in America where, by the 1890s, Brownells, a large tour operator, relied on local travel agents throughout the United States to sell their tours.

Opposite From their earliest days Cooks used the power of advertising to promote new ideas.

American Express in Paris: the famous office at 11, rue Scribe. *Below* Inside, comfortable armchairs, reading tables and daily newspapers made it more like a club than a travel agent's office.

'All part of the service' was a phrase open to generous interpretation by early travel agents. American Express entered the travel business in earnest in 1915. One of their most famous offices was (and still is) at 11, rue Scribe in Paris. During the 1920s writers and artists used it as their club and about ten thousand letters arrived there daily for clients who were staying in Paris or elsewhere in Europe. As Hitler marched into European countries American Express and Thomas Cooks helped thousands of refugees to escape. In the chaos following the Second World War the travel agent had some extraordinary assignments. American Express found themselves responsible for hundreds of barking duffel bags. When the last shot had been fired and the troops left for the United States, many GIs turned up at embarkation points with loyal canine friends concealed in their kit bags. The dogs were mostly

strays who had befriended American troops and
accompanied them through the horrors of war.
The dogs weren't allowed on troopships but were
entrusted to American Express to deliver to their
owners once they had got home.

Affairs of the heart are not unknown to travel
agents in the 1990s either: in the middle of a

During the 1920s business travellers took advantage of improved
facilities on the railways: businessmen and women relax in the
lounge of the LMS 'Royal Scot', 1928.

recent travel consultation a young man proposed
to his girlfriend and the travel consultant was
asked to arrange the wedding in Mauritius. Things
don't always work out as well as that: 'Dear Sir,'
wrote a client to a Thomas Cook branch manager
in 1965, 'Will you please cancel travel
arrangements made by Mr —— for October 3rd as
the wedding has been cancelled because he is
already married.'

The travel agency industry has changed
drastically since Thomas Cook's own day.
Throughout the 1960s, '70s and '80s there were
many mergers, acquisitions and failures among
travel agents. Recession and structural changes in
the industry squeezed out many of the smaller

agencies, leaving Thomas Cook, American Express, Wagons-Lits and Carlson as the pre-eminent players in the global market. Umbrella organizations like the Association of British Travel Agents (ABTA), founded in 1950, and the World Tourism Organization (WTO) based in Madrid, monitor and help the industry and its consumers. The services offered by travel agents today are complex and backed by sophisticated new technology. It is now possible to make a booking

or get a ticket printed in your office or at your hotel; there are increasingly sophisticated computer systems to help the traveller get the best value and convenience in their travel arrangements. And of course there is that ubiquitous piece of plastic, the credit card. It is already possible to book a holiday direct from your sitting room by picking up the phone, and in some countries, people can already reserve the holiday of their dreams through their home computer.

Competition between rival travel companies has always been intense and one of the reasons for Thomas Cook's early success was his realization that marketing was very important. As a printer he understood the power of the printed word and

No time to waste: a 1920s typist takes dictation as the train speeds to the next business meeting. *Inset* In the 1990s sophisticated computer systems at one of Thomas Cooks' Travel Management Centres provide the traveller with the latest travel information.

The Excursionist, renamed the *Traveller's Gazette* in 1903, was the first
travel magazine.

issued handbills to advertise his earliest tours. In the following decades Cook's eye-catching posters and brochure covers set the travel industry's style for selling dreams, as did his first travel magazine *The Excursionist* which gave details of Cook's tours and was published regularly in worldwide editions for almost a century. On the first world tour in 1872–3 Thomas Cook filed several reports of his travels to *The Times* in a series called 'Letters from the Sea and from Foreign Lands'. While he wrote about the real thing, Jules Verne's fictional tour, *Round the World in Eighty Days* was serialized in a Parisian newspaper.

Publishing and the media still play a very important role in the travel industry. The traveller today is bombarded with information about travelling: there are special supplements in newspapers, specialist magazines, television and radio programmes and videos. Each year thousands of new travel and guidebooks are published: there are Red, Green and Blue guides, rough guides, city guides, travel-on-the-cheap guides; there are even guides which tell you how to read an airline ticket. Future generations will probably publish guides to the galaxy. Guides for the business traveller abound; they cover every aspect of business life from hotels with the best business facilities to etiquette in distant lands. Among the first series of guidebooks published were those of Baedeker and of John Murray who published a two volume eight hundred-page *Handbook for London* in 1849 – not exactly a pocket guide. These early nineteenth-century guidebooks are now collectors' items.

In the thirteenth century Marco Polo did not have the help of a guidebook. He found the time to write about his travels when he was a prisoner-of-war years after his great journey through the Hindu Kush, the Pamirs, Kashgar, Yarkand and the Gobi Desert to reach Beijing in search of trade in 1275. Although this incredible business trip made the young Venetian merchant the most famous of all business travellers he was not the first to trade with China. Roman Legions guarding Hadrian's Wall in the north of England carried banners made of Chinese silk, so some enterprising businessman had seized trading opportunities centuries before Marco Polo.

The business traveller has been trotting the globe for centuries; before the nineteenth century most travel was for business purposes. Elizabeth I gave business travel allowances to young, aspiring courtiers so that they could travel throughout Europe making important contacts useful to their careers and to their queen. George III irritated American colonists by summoning them to meetings in 'places unusual, uncomfortable and distant' – a complaint familiar to many of today's business executives.

Until the nineteenth century, Marco Polo's account of his travels in Asia and China, which he dictated between 1296 and 1298, was virtually the only source of information about the Far East.

Mr Pilkington of the English glass firm had an important meeting in Paris on 15 July 1919, but he had missed the boat-train and thought he had missed the meeting. On the evening of 14 July he was flicking through the *London Evening News* when he spotted an article which said that the ban on commercial flights between Britain and the rest of

The first flying commercial traveller: a salesman loads a sample of the Tellus Super Vacuum Cleaner onto an aeroplane ready for a sales trip throughout the UK, 1926.

Europe had been lifted. He immediately chartered a plane to take him to Paris the next day and made his meeting. Mr Pilkington was delighted and became such an enthusiast for air travel that he went on to make many more business trips by air, some of them as far afield as Australia. He was the first British businessman to take advantage of air travel, although many of the early passengers flew for business reasons.

In recent years there has been an explosion in the growth of business travel. As you board any European airline shuttle you may see cabin crew hurriedly moving the cabin dividers to make more seats available in business class, knowing that greater profits can be made from this sector.

It is estimated that business travel (both national and international) accounted for 750 million trips worldwide in 1989 and was probably worth about $320 billion. About one in five of all trips are made for business purposes and the business travel industry is growing at twice the speed of tourism. British and American companies are reported to spend more on travel and entertainment than on advertising and promotion or corporate taxes. Companies in the UK are reputed to have spent about £22 billion on travel and entertainment in 1990.

This phenomenon affects all areas of the travel industry: the airlines, most of which had introduced some sort of business class travel by the mid-seventies, now sell about 50 per cent of all scheduled flight tickets to business travellers. Some airlines provide in-flight phone, fax, telex and mail services to help working travellers, and to attract the lucrative business market. Without the custom of the conference delegate, salesman or business executive, many hotels would close. Most large corporations have dedicated staff responsible for organizing and controlling business travel and expenditure and most major travel companies have departments which deal exclusively with the business traveller.

Late one night the telephone rang at the 24-hour office of a business travel company in London. An agitated businessman at the other end of the line complained that a water pipe was leaking in his hotel room. The travel consultant on duty asked where he was ringing from. 'Los Angeles' replied the voice. Swallowing hard the consultant patiently suggested that he contact hotel reception for help; an idea that hadn't occurred to the businessman. On another occasion a client rang in to say that he had left an extremely expensive bottle of perfume on the plane. It was a birthday present for his wife, could the business travel team retrieve it for him? The team went into action but drew a surprising blank. Just as they were puzzling over the next move the man rang back to tell them that they were on a wild goose chase. He explained that there never had been a bottle of perfume, but he had made the first call in front of his wife who was now quite happy because she thought her husband had merely left her birthday present behind, not, as he had actually done, completely forgotten her birthday.

These are extreme cases, but competition for business clients between travel companies is keen and the services laid on for business travellers are considerable and proclaimed through high pressure marketing. There is a move towards providing an integrated package of services for corporate clients, generally termed travel management. They range from 24-hour, 365-day

Business colleagues work on board an InterCity 125.

booking services to trouble-shooting units manned by experienced travel consultants who can conjure up a private jet at three o'clock in the morning. Business travel companies can help clients to keep a check on expenditure by providing a detailed breakdown of how much money they are spending on travel. They also keep details on computer of

Business travellers are important customers to the travel trade, and keep the airlines busy; about half of all airline scheduled flight tickets are sold to business travellers. *Inset* A transatlantic corporate business jet.

their clients' individual preferences for particular hire cars, hotels, airlines, aircraft seats and types of food, so that whenever possible their needs are met. Some travel companies have business centres at major airports where scurrying executives can make use of work stations, business machines, meeting-rooms and secretarial services, while waiting for flights.

In New York and Boston businessmen and women can get business travel advice and tips on how to keep travelling costs down by tuning in to daily business travel programmes on local radio stations. Technology is speeding processes all the time: clients of Thomas Cook Travel in the US can get direct information about flights and make bookings without going through a travel consultant or speaking to anyone at an airline. They dial a special number which faxes flight information to them, they can then book a flight direct – all accomplished, as the publicity hand-outs say, in three minutes using 'phone, fax and finger'.

Twenty years ago the sight of Japanese tourists lounging in the tropical garden of a Balinese hotel roused curiosity, especially since the Japanese did not travel much for pleasure in those days, and these tourists were only in Bali for the weekend. They were, in fact, star workers whose performance on the shop floor was being rewarded with a weekend in paradise. Incentive travel is now huge business: the most recently available figures estimate it to be worth over $2 billion yearly in the US and about £400 million yearly in the UK. To reach or exceed tough targets, an executive's company may offer the incentive of a holiday abroad if he or she succeeds, and so the business executive adds to the swelling tide of international tourists.

During the 1980s the number of Japanese tourists increased by 133 per cent; the number of Americans travelling abroad reached over forty-one million, although this was a relatively small percentage of the population; over 70 per cent of British adults had been abroad (mostly on package holidays), but West Germany was the major tourist-generating country.

These industrialized countries have people with the time and money to travel. Their destinations are often countries which have excellent weather, beautiful beaches and scenery and abundant wildlife, but few other resources. To some of these countries tourism has become very big business indeed: it is the main source of income and the driving force behind the national economy. The business of travel is vital to the economic survival of such countries, but as the numbers of tourists and travellers increase, a compromise has to be reached between the identity of the host country and the 'golden hordes' of tourists which threaten to swamp it and destroy the very characteristics which make it so attractive in the first place. In the meantime, many hope that the world travel industry, conservationists and national governments will together strive to achieve this balance.

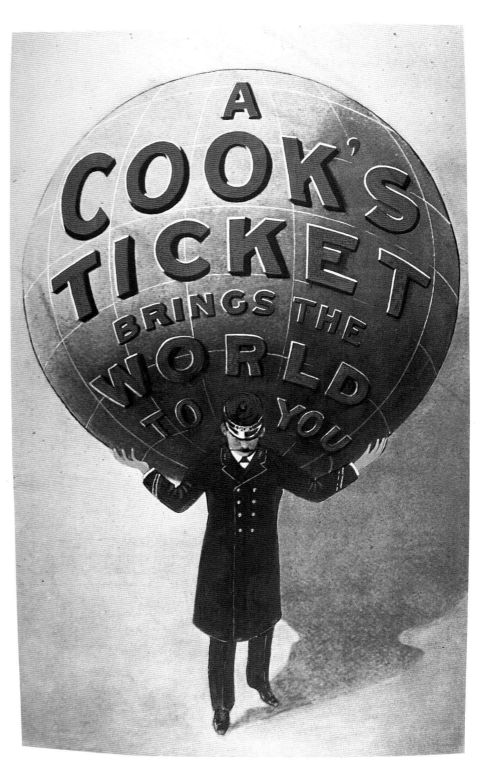

An early Thomas Cook poster.

CHAPTER 7

At Home and Abroad

THERE IS A CREEK in North America which in early summer is overhung with arching fronds of flowers; you have to duck in and out of them as you paddle the canoe. Eventually it reaches an open stretch of water which mirrors forests, mountains and the vast sky. The liquid picture is pierced by petrified trees and paddling between the towering, upturned roots and the column-like trunks is as haunting as a visit to a sunken city. On the far side of a beaver dam, clouds of dragonflies hover and swerve above an escaping tumble of water. To a town dweller the silence is eerie – so this is how the wilderness felt to the early explorers and settlers. No wonder only 10 per cent of American adults have a valid passport; why bother to go abroad when you have all this at home.

To European eyes it may seem that in summer their cities and beauty spots are overrun by Daughters of the Revolution in trainers and beige macks, but most Americans take their holidays in America. They've been doing so since bathing machines first appeared on Long Island in about 1794. At the beginning of the nineteenth century the East Coast resorts such as Newport, Long Branch, Cape May, Bar Harbor and Saratoga Springs were the places to see and be seen, but by the 1880s Atlantic City was the most popular seaside resort.

Contrary to the celluloid image, the West was not all dust and sweat. Once the railroad had reached the West Coast, grand hotels like the Del Monte in Monterey, opened in 1880, attracted hundreds of visitors with its pinnacles and porticos, games room, restaurants, botanical gardens and maze. Florida was opened up as a

Atlantic City's vast beach and boardwalk made it the American seaside resort of the nineteenth century.

Opposite A mirror lake in Yosemite National Park.

winter resort in the 1890s by Henrys Flagler and Plant, both millionaires and railroad company owners.

Although the inland wonders of the North American continent were well known to hunters and fishermen, it was the railroad which brought areas of the Rocky Mountains and the Sierra Nevada within reach of people of more moderate means. With astonishing foresight Yellowstone was opened as a National Park as early as 1872. Yosemite followed in 1890, but one of the wonders of the natural world remained fairly remote from the public until the turn of the century – the Grand Canyon was not made a National Park until 1906. By 1981 there were so many people wanting to raft through the Canyon on the Colorado River that there was an eight-year waiting-list and places now have to be decided by a once-a-year lottery. Ninety per cent of the places go to package rafting firms which means that independent spirits cannot pit themselves against the boiling waters of the Colorado.

Opposite One of the natural wonders of the world, the Grand Canyon attracts huge numbers of tourists to Arizona.

'The lakes of Switzerland would be buffalo wallows in Texas' wrote Will Rogers. 'There is single ranches here bigger than France.' The United States is so big that even in the twentieth century the inhabitants prefer to explore their own

Idyllic Kennedy Meadows in the Sierra Nevada, USA. Why travel further? *Inset* This 1950s travel brochure put remote Alaska on the tourist map.

Overleaf Not so famous but also spectacular: Bryce Canyon in Utah.

continent. About 120 thousand Americans
travelled to Europe in 1900 and by 1990 that
figure had reached 7 million, but in the same year
about 14 million US citizens travelled to Mexico
and 13.4 million to Canada. Market research
showed that only 15 per cent of US adults had
made a 'foreign' trip in the three years prior to

Adventurous British travellers discovered many new destinations:
a party of Victorians try Japanese transport.

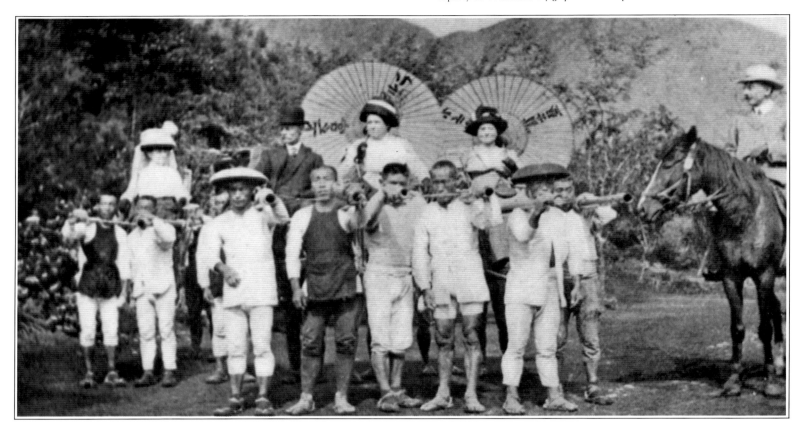

1989 – and that included trips to Hawaii and
Alaska.

The French also like to stay at home and prefer
to take their leisure in their own country. If they
do travel abroad their main destinations are Spain
and Italy. The Scandinavians like to travel south
to the warmth of the Mediterranean, so do
50 per cent of the British who go abroad for their
holidays, although they also like to cross the
'herring pond' and explore the United States. By
far the biggest travellers and spenders on travel
are the Germans; 60 per cent of them go abroad
for their holidays, mostly to Spain, Italy or
Austria.

It wasn't always so. During the second half of
the nineteenth century the British were constantly
discovering new holiday destinations. They
travelled to Switzerland in droves, swarming over
the mountain passes. Tightly corsetted women,
holding parasols aloft, traipsed across glaciers and
climbed mountains in the dark before dawn to
watch the sun rise from the top. The first Cook's
tour to Switzerland in 1863 is on official record as
an important contribution to the start of the Swiss
tourist industry. The British tourists also made

Fastidiously-dressed Victorian tourists silhouetted against the
glare of a Swiss glacier.

Egypt peculiarly their own. There are many nineteenth-century journals describing Nile cruises and trips to climb the pyramids. Thackeray rather irritably described the view after an undignified scramble to the top '. . . no better . . . than you beheld from the bottom; only a little more river, and sand, and ricefield'.

The sun, sea and sand mentality of the 1960s and '70s package holiday-maker would have shocked Victorian and Edwardian tourists, who travelled mainly for self improvement. There were some departures from the norm: just after the First World War several tour operators organized trips to the battlefields of France and Belgium. Some tourists went to tramp through the ruined fields of the Somme in genuine homage to the memory of those who had died, but others went to gawp. For the most part, however, early tourists stuck to monuments, museums, churches and works of art. The Alps were compelling, but only as part of the scenery, not as the winter activity playground they were to become.

Centre Since the second half of the nineteenth century the spell of the pyramids has drawn tourists, especially the British, to Egypt. *Inset top* Monumental pillars of the Ancient Egyptian temple at Karnak, Luxor. *Inset below* Pulled and pushed tourists made the rather undignified scramble up the pyramids in the nineteenth century.

Skiing was one of the best-kept secrets in the world until Mathias Zdarsky invented downhill or Alpine skiing and opened the first real ski school near Vienna by the beginning of the twentieth century. The very first school was, believe it or not, in Australia where a Norwegian taught the miners of the Snowy Mountains how to slide on

Sir Henry Lunn (*seated, centre front row*) organized the first winter sports package tour to Chamonix in 1898/9. *Inset* Alpine skiing began as a winter sport at the turn of the century and today accounts for billions in tourism revenue.

skis as early as 1861. Of course the Scandinavians have been skiing for about 4,500 years, but they used it as a means of travelling across country, not as an activity in itself, that has only happened in the last hundred years. Today the skiing industry is worth billions and there are more than three thousand resorts catering for about thirty million skiers across the world.

The first Alpine skiers were regarded as rather eccentric, but the sport gradually took hold where there were already mountain resorts such as Davos in Switzerland. The tour operator, Sir Henry Lunn, founded the Public Schools Alpine Sports Club in 1902 and began the British passion for speeding down the piste. By the 1920s the Swiss jokingly complained that they needed a passport to enter some parts of their country because British skiers had taken them over, and by 1921 there were few Alpine slopes, skiable with contemporary equipment, which had not been tried out by enthusiasts.

The new sport was hard work. There were no ski-lifts so those who wanted higher slopes than the nurseries rose early and carrying all their gear – wire for repairs, spare sealskin gloves, sweaters and food – in a rucksack, climbed for three or four hours and then skied down, reaching the village by twilight, just in time to change for *après-ski* activities. Once the T-bar drag-lift had been invented and installed in Davos in 1934, it was possible to get to runs, which had previously taken a twenty-minute climb to reach, in half a minute. Remote villages could join in the skiing bonanza because they could be reached by drag-lifts, which were much cheaper to install than railways or funiculars. As more villages were opened to skiers the sport became cheaper, and a greater variety of people were able to join the affluent elitists on the slopes.

In America there was and is far less formality. The world's first chair-lift was installed in Sun Valley, Idaho in 1934 – a resort designed by Hollywood architects who copied, but had never been to, the Tyrol. Skiing in the Rockies is a pleasant mix of downhill and cross-country and there is far less snobbery towards that ancient form of skiing. European *pistes* are becoming more and more overcrowded and there is a move away from the endless queues for the ski-lifts. Adventurous skiers in search of new experiences are shunning the drag-lifts and climbing the slopes themselves. Cross-country skiing is also enjoying a revival.

Paid holidays, more affluence and cheaper travel have turned the last few decades into an era of travel. But for many, travel for travel's sake is not enough. People want to travel to pursue their hobbies, or try new ones, and the specialist tour operators have responded with a plethora of organized activities. Trampolining in Outer Mongolia may not be your heart's desire, but there are plenty of others to choose from. It is possible to indulge a passion for military history, bridge, or photography in beautiful surroundings thousands of miles from home, with resident experts as guides and teachers. You can learn to paint at the foot of Cezanne's Mont Sainte-Victoire, to cook in Umbria, to ride in the Rockies, meditate in Andalucia, or to skin-dive in the Caribbean.

St Andrew's Golf Club, near New York, was founded in 1888 and today most American resorts have a golf course. Amateur golfers travel to play, searching out the most challenging courses around the world. Soccer and football enthusiasts travel across continents to follow and support their teams, and there are countless organized holidays on which the client can learn any sport from

Skiing became a chic and popular holiday for women.

archery to flotilla sailing and wind surfing.

'Safety helmets and wet suits are essential, you must be able to swim and it's vital to follow the leader's instructions immediately, above all, hang on . . . packed lunches are included . . .' It doesn't sound like a picnic, much less a holiday, but the leaflet helps to prime novices at white water rafting. Adventure holidays are increasingly popular and the brave can test their physical and mental endurance in a number of ways from outward-bound courses where the participants usually spend the last few days of their 'holiday' building themselves a shelter in a sodden landscape and living off nature, to dog-sledging across the Arctic Circle and learning how to build an igloo on the way.

The adventurous can also canoe down the Amazon, trek through the Patagonian uplands, explore volcano craters, or sail round Cape Horn in a square rigger. Skiing adventurers have taken to heli-skiing which involves learning to operate an electronic transmitter in case of avalanches. The heli-skier is lifted into remote parts of mountain ranges which other skiers cannot reach, in the Alps, Sweden, the Himalayas and in New Zealand, and left to ski across unknown terrain which makes black runs look like nursery slopes.

In Africa adventure comes on safari. Travelling across parts of the great continent by 4-wheel drive vehicle, camel, balloon or even on foot, the aim is to see as much of Africa's wildlife as possible. The best chance is often away from the tourist lodges on a tented safari and although wildlife programmes on television are enthralling viewing, nothing beats the excitement of seeing a live leopard in the headlights or an elephant at a waterhole. It makes your heart beat at an invigorating pace.

Flicking through the travel brochures the browser is confronted by an astonishing number of photographs of whales' flukes. There is a bewildering array of environmental and wildlife holidays to choose from. The real enthusiast has been doing it for years. Like the ornithologist who has to reach an impossibly remote island by a certain day in the rainy season only to find it overflowing with ornithologists from all over the world choking the woodland tracks with cameras and tripods, trying to catch a fleeting glimpse of a small bird as it hops about in the dripping undergrowth. But for the interested amateur the travel companies offer trips which include opportunities to follow the grey whales of the San Ignacio Lagoon, view tigers in India, search for orchids and birds of paradise in Papua New Guinea, or track down the gorillas in the Mountains of the Moon. It is even possible to take a package holiday to view a total eclipse of the sun wherever there is a chance to see it (Hawaii, 1991).

White water rafting on the River Tully in North Queensland, Australia. *Inset* Diving lesson on the Great Barrier Reef.

Although the only shots taken on safari these days are with cameras, not with rifles, irresponsible tourism can be a threat to conservation. In some parts of African game reserves, such as the Masai Mara, it is not unusual to come across dozens of tourist trucks jostling for the best position to view game.

They churn up the ground, scare away the wildlife and drive across the scrub flattening cover for the animals. Responsible tour operators have recognized the problem and are doing all in their power to stop it. Many employ highly qualified environmentalists to lead their tours. Some advertise their trips as environmental journeys and have hit on an ingenious method of sponsorship. For each trip booked the travel organization contributes to a conservation programme, such as buying an acre of rainforest, sponsoring research into whales and dolphins, or funding anti-poaching programmes in the Masai Mara or Serengeti. It is, as yet, a small contribution, but it is an important beginning for, as travel companies realize, without the environments and the animal and plant life they support, there will be no point in travelling to see them.

Travel has also long been associated with health. The Romans used spas and bathed in warm spring waters wherever they could find them. They even found them in Britain, and Bath remained a watering place for centuries. It was especially popular in the late eighteenth and early

Centre Penguins size up a tourist in Antarctica. *Inset top* From the safety of a safari truck, a tourist is confronted by a lion on his home territory. *Above* Mountain walking in the Dolomites.

An early form of health club? Floating trays of refreshments and card games at a nineteenth-century Swiss spa.

nineteenth centuries when the whole of
fashionable society decamped from London to
Bath once a year to take the waters and to see and
be seen. The fashion for spas has died out in
Britain, but in Germany and Italy there are still
spas where people gather to drink the waters and
undergo hydrotherapies.

The sea, too, was considered good for health
and the fashion for sea bathing was originally for
health reasons rather than for a jolly seaside
holiday. Victorian doctors often recommended a
cruise as a cure for prolonged ailments because
the sea air was considered to be an excellent aid
to recovery. The Victorians also realized the
beneficial effects of mountain air. Resorts such as
Davos in Switzerland were started as health
resorts for tuberculosis sufferers. Davos
accommodated several hundred tuberculosis
patients and their supporting relatives long before
Alpine skiing was invented. Although very few
people today travel specifically for their health, in
many societies holidays are considered essential to
both mental and physical well being.

A recent American survey has shown that most

Children in Edwardian England enjoying the sea air below
Bamburgh Castle, Northumbria.

people travel to escape from something. Many
professional travellers say that there is nowhere
left to travel, but for most of us the old maxim
that anywhere is new if you have not been there
before, is true, and there are plenty of places left

to escape to. It is often said, for example, that the Indonesian island of Bali is ruined and that it hasn't been worth going to since the 1930s, but to walk through a Balinese night breathing the warm silk of tropical air accompanied by the croaking of frogs and the distant gongs and gamelan music of a temple celebration is a magical experience. In

Although Bali is a mecca for tourists, its culture and beauty survive.

spite of an overdose of tourism the essential spirit of Bali is still alive.

There is much to see and beach package holidays are no longer sufficient to satisfy the curious traveller. Since the last World War people are travelling at a much younger age. In Europe many children have visited another country before their tenth birthday, and generations have grown

up with the expectation of travel. Over the last
two decades people have become increasingly
adventurous, less prejudiced and more
knowledgeable about travel. Today it is possible to
experience places and events which even thirty
years ago could only be seen on the pages of
geography textbooks. Travel is so much the norm

Iguazu Falls, 2,470 metres wide, on the borders of Argentina,
Brazil and Paraguay.

that even family celebrations such as marriage
have become part of the travel business. Some
travel brochures have special wedding sections –
couples can travel thousands of miles from home
in order to get married in an exotic location.
Travel companies will arrange weddings which
include the ceremony, the cake, flowers,
buttonholes, photographer and even a best man if
necessary, in places like the Seychelles or the
Caribbean.

Whatever the style of travel – as an independent
traveller or in an organized group – there is a
kaleidoscope of destinations waiting to be reached.
The street of the storytellers in Peshawar,
Pakistan; a desert island in the Indian Ocean, the
magnificent Iguazu Falls in Argentina, the Potala
in Tibet and the gigantic statues of Easter Island
had, until recently, been seen by few people other
than the local population, explorers, archaeol-
ogists or anthropologists, yet they are all included
in the pages of current travel brochures.

Tourists can now marvel first hand at the mysterious statues on
Easter Island.

CHAPTER 8

Beyond the Horizon

'SINCE LIFE IS SO SHORT and the world is wide, the sooner you start exploring it the better . . . Go now', the writer Simon Raven advised students in 1968. Young people who took his excellent advice played their part in the incredible escalation of the numbers of people travelling over the last few decades. Before 1939 the number of international travellers was estimated to be about one million a year, estimates for the year 2000 vary between 600 thousand million and 2 billion. The most recent estimates from the World Tourism Organization puts the number of people travelling nationally and internationally at 3.5 billion every year. It's quite a thought that some of the biggest nations on earth – USSR, China, India – have not yet begun mass international travel.

Many will be business travellers, some tourists and others simply travellers and most of them will come, as they do now, from the affluent countries of Europe, North America and Australasia. As holiday allowances, personal incomes and life expectancy rise in these countries there will be more time and more money to spend on travel. A new kind of tourist, a hybrid of the traveller and the tourist, is already beginning to emerge. The students of the 1960s and their children are more widely travelled than previous generations, they are also more aware of the environment and of other cultures and are generally more analytical. They are beginning to reject the shrink-wrapped mentality of the mass tourist, they want to travel further and more independently, and the travel industry has already begun to adapt to their needs by tailoring individual travel arrangements and giving a more personal service.

But will much of the world be open to them, or

Opposite Space shuttle: tickets have already been reserved on commercial space flights of the future.

Ayers Rock at sunset. Sacred to Aborigines and a focus of Australian tourism, the monolith stands within the protecting boundaries of Uluru National Park. *Inset* Traditional reed boat on Lake Titicaca, Bolivia.

Overleaf Hong Kong by night. The future of this city, for business and travel, may well change when it reverts to China in 1997.

The spectacular ice cave on Ross Island, Antarctica. There is international concern that the delicate ecological balance of this great wilderness could be harmed by tourism. *Inset* The Parthenon, Athens, a casualty of mass tourism.

will they have to put their names down for the seats which some travel companies, like Thomas Cook, have already reserved on future space flights for the first holiday on the Moon? In East Berlin, the government recognized the power of travel and the way in which it can change ideas and perceptions, and enclosed its people within a concrete wall. The *cri de coeur* of the East Berliners was that they longed to be allowed travel. At the time none of them had any idea that their dream would come true, yet the Berlin Wall came down and East Berliners could freely cross into West Berlin and travel beyond too. The countries of Eastern Europe, previously closed to travellers from the West, are now anxious to attract tourists and the foreign currency which they bring. The world seems to open and close. As one country shuts down its borders through war or politics, another opens its doors to travellers.

The sheer numbers of people travelling has created an international debate about the future of tourism and its effect on the world. Mass tourism is already beginning to threaten the existence of the things it loves: the Parthenon, worn away by too many feet; the Sistine chapel in danger from the heat of too many bodies; the cave paintings of Lascaux attacked by mould through too much breath and bacteria. Whole environments can also be endangered by tourism: the Alps and the Mediterranean, two of the world's most fragile ecosystems have already been damaged by it.

Many developing countries are anxious to use their natural resources of beautiful beaches, scenery and rich cultural life to attract tourism and its attendant affluence. But unless it is sympathetically and rigorously controlled tourism can have a disastrous effect. At its very worst it can 'trinketize' cultures, reduce the local cuisine to hamburgers and cola and turn hospitality into hustling. It's quite possible to swamp a small country with a tourist industry so that all its traditions and culture are lost and it becomes a nation of waiters living in tourist resorts. Tourism can bring great economic benefits to emerging nations, but ensuring that such countries get a slice of the tourist cake while at the same time protecting the local way of life is a delicate balancing act which governments, developers and tour operators must urgently perfect.

Green tourism which takes care of cultures and environments is a great challenge for the future. There are several ways in which the incentives and economic benefits of tourism can enhance development. Many buildings and monuments of great historical value have been restored. Tourists to Rwanda have helped to protect the gorillas because they have made the animals the country's greatest source of foreign currency. It is in Florida's interest to protect some of its reefs

Tourism needs to be well-planned to bring benefits to a nation's economy and its environment. A hotel complex in Mauritius.
Inset Hawkers ply their wares along the Puno–Cuzco railway, Peru.

because they attract so many tourists who bring
fifty million dollars a year to just one of Florida's
counties.

Travel has great potential for good. It increases
our knowledge of the world, changes perceptions
and brings greater understanding between
peoples. A journey distances us from the
complicated tangles of our lives and gives us the
opportunity to grasp more balanced proportions
and wider perspectives. Its challenges can increase
our knowledge of ourselves. It can also be
extremely relaxing and enormous fun. So whether
a traveller chooses the security of organized travel
or the mysteries of the independent journey, it is
important to pack the bags and go. 'I shall
find . . . above all, things wonderful and
fascinating innumerable.' Kipling's words were
written about India, but they equally apply to the
rest of the world about us.

Journey's end: Nagin Lake, Kashmir.

Travel brings greater understanding of peoples and cultures: a
library in Tikse, Ladakh.

Opposite Thousands of tourists visit the Taj Mahal annually but it
retains its serene splendour. Tourism at such monuments requires
careful management so that future generations can wonder at
them too.

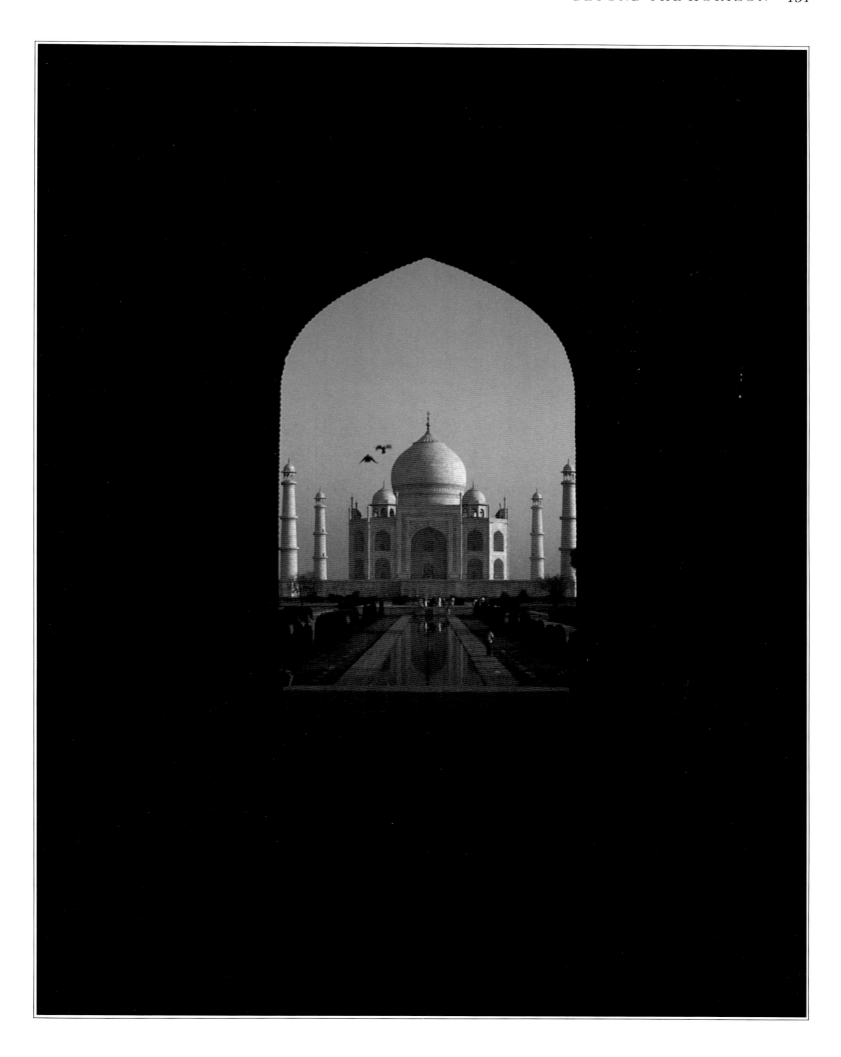

THE TRAVELLER'S GAZETTE.

An Illustrated Journal Devoted to Travel

Published Monthly
by
THOS. COOK & SON

CHIEF OFFICE
LUDGATE CIRCUS, LONDON, E.C.

Sources

Allen, Charles, *Plain Tales From The Raj*. Andre
  Deutsch/BBC, 1975

American Express, *American Express in Europe*

Barron, James and Tubbs, D.B., *Vintage Cars in
  Colour*. Batsford, 1960

Basho, Matsuo, *The Narrow Road to the Deep North*.
  Penguin, 1966

Beeb, Lucius, *The Big Spenders*. Hutchinson, 1966

Behrend, George and Buchanon, Gary, *Night Ferry*.
  Jersey Artists, 1975

Bird Bishop, Isabella, *A Lady's Life in the Rocky
  Mountains*. Murray, 1879

Bonnington, Chris, *Quest For Adventure*. Hodder and
  Stoughton, 1981

Bray, Winston, *The History of BOAC*. BOAC

British Airways, *Highways in the Air, The story of BA*.
  BA, 1979

Burgess, Alan, *The Small Woman*. Evans, 1969

Burkardt, A.J., and Medlik S.A., *Tourism Past,
  Present and Future*. Heinemann, 1974

—— *Tourism*. Heinemann, 1981

Burton, Isabel, *The Life of Richard Burton*. London,
  1893

Burton, Sir Richard Francis, *The Lake Regions of
  Central Africa*. London, 1860

—— *The Personal Narrative of a Pilgrimage to El
  Medinah and Mecca*. London, 1855

Byron, Robert, *The Road to Oxiana*. Macmillan, 1937

Cable, Boyd, *A Hundred Year History of the P & O
  Steam Navigation Company*. Nicholson and Watson,
  1937

Caillié, Réné, *Travels through Central Africa to
  Timbuktoo*. Vol. 2, 1830

Cook, Thomas Ltd, *European Timetable, 1990*

—— *Overseas Timetable, 1990*

—— *The Excursionist*

—— *The Traveller's Gazette*

—— *Time Traveller*

Cookridge, E.H., *The Orient Express*. Allen Lane,
  1979

WINTER SPORTS
IN
NORTH DERBYSHIRE.

In the clear bracing air of North Derbyshire, where fogs are unknown, you will find all the winter through something to amuse you. Good Golf and Motoring, or Hunting with the High Peak. Lovers of high-class music will appreciate the Pavilion Concerts in the evening, and theatre-goers will find good companies playing at the new Opera House.

To those who like Switzerland, BUXTON in snow is specially attractive. They understand winter sports there, and ski-ing, curling, sleighing and skating get into full swing directly the winter comes.

TRY A WEEK-END AT BUXTON.

David-Neel, Alexandra, *My Journey to Lhasa.* Heinemann, 1927

Davidson, Lilias Campbell, *Hints to Lady Travellers.* London, 1893

Davidson, Robyn, *Tracks.* Cape, 1980

Dodwell, Christina, *Travels with Fortune.* W.H. Allen, 1979

—— *In Papua New Guinea.* Oxford Illustrated Press, 1983

Edwards, Amelia B., *A Thousand Miles Up The Nile.* Longmans, 1888

Feiffer, Maxine, *Going Places.* Macmillan, 1985

Fermor, Patrick Leigh, *The Traveller's Tree.* John Murray, 1950

Fiennes, Celia, *Through England on a Side Saddle.* London, 1888

Fishlock, Trevor, *India File.* John Murray, 1983

Fleming, Peter, *News From Tartary.* Cape, 1936

Fraser, John Foster, *Round the World on a Wheel.* London, 1899

Gill, Chris (ed.), *The Good Skiing Guide.* The Consumers' Association and Hodder and Stoughton, 1988

Gwynn, Stephen, *The Life of Mary Kingsley.* Macmillan, 1933

Girl's Own Annual, Collections of *The Girl's Own Paper,* 1887, 1888, 1889, 1890, 1891, 1901

Harrer, Heinrich, *Seven Years in Tibet.* Hart-David, 1953

Harrison, Rose, *My Life In Service.* Cassell, 1975

Heath, Lady Mary and Wolfe, Stella, *Woman and Flying.* Longman, 1929

Heyerdahl, Thor, *The Kon-Tiki Expedition.* Allen and Unwin, 1950

Hibbert, Christopher, *The Grand Tour.* Spring Books, 1974

—— *The English, A Social History.* Grafton Books, 1987

Hindley, *Tourists, Travellers and Pilgrims.* Hutchinson, 1983

Howarth, David and Stephen, *The Story of P & O.* Weidenfeld and Nicholson, 1986

Hudson, Kenneth and Pettifer, Julian, *Diamonds In The Sky.* The Bodley Head/BBC, 1979

Hudson, Kenneth, *Air Travel, A Social History.* Adams and Dart, 1972

Jefferies, Susan (ed.), *Travelling Light, Punch Goes Abroad.* Punch/Grafton Books, 1988

Keay, John, *Into India.* Charles Scribner, 1973

Kemble, Fanny, *Records of a Girlhood.* Beckes, 1878

—— *Records of a Later Life.* Bentley, 1882

—— *Further Records.* Bentley, 1890

Kennedy, Ludovic, *A Book of Railway Journeys.* Collins, 1980

Kingsley, Mary, *Travels in West Africa.* Macmillan, 1897

Lacey, Robert, *The Queens of the North Atlantic.* Sidgwick and Jackson, 1973

Livingstone, David, *Missionary Travels and Researches in South Africa.* London, 1860

Marsden-Smedley, Philip and Klinke, Jeffrey (ed.), *Views From Abroad, The Spectator Book of Travel Writing*. Grafton Books, 1988

Matthieson, Peter, *The Snow Leopard*. Chatto and Windus, 1979

Middleton, Dorothy, *Victorian Lady Travellers*. Routledge and Kegan Paul, 1965

Morrell, Jemima, *Miss Jemima's Swiss Journal*. Putnam & Sons, 1963

Morris, Christopher (ed.), *Journeys of Celia Fiennes*. Cresset Press, 1947

Morris, Jan, *Journeys*. Oxford University Press, 1984

Moynahan, Brian, *Airport International*. Macmillan, 1978

Murphy, Dervla, *Full Tilt*. John Murray, 1965
—— *Wheels Within Wheels*. John Murray, 1979

Newby, Eric, *A Short Walk in the Hindu Kush*. Secker and Warberg, 1972
—— *A Traveller's Life*. Collins, 1982
—— *Traveller's Tales*. Collins, 1985

Norwich, John Julius, *A Taste for Travel*. Macmillan, 1985

O'Hanlon, Redmond, *Into the Heart of Borneo*. Penguin Books, 1985
—— *In Trouble Again*. Hamish Hamilton, 1988

Owen, Charles, *The Grand Days of Travel*. Webb and Bower, 1979

Page, Martin, *The Lost Pleasures of the Great Trains*. Weidenfeld and Nicholson, 1975

The Paston Letters. Oxford University Press, 1983

Padfield, Peter, *Beneath the House Flag of the P & O*. Hutchinson, 1981

Philips-Birt, Douglas, *When Luxury Went to Sea*. David and Charles, 1971

Post, Emily, *Etiquette*. Funk and Wagnalls, 1922

Pudney, John, *The Thomas Cook Story*. Michael Joseph, 1953

Quest, Miles (ed.), *Horwath Book of Tourism*. Macmillan, 1990

Rentell, Philip, *Historic Cunard Liners*. Atlantic Transport Publishers, 1986

Robertson, Patrick, *The Shell Book of Firsts*. Ebury Press and Michael Joseph, 1983

Robinson, Jane, *Wayward Women: A Guide to Women Travellers*. Oxford University Press, 1990

Russell, Mary, *The Blessings of a Good Thick Skirt*. Collins, 1988

Sales, H. Pearce (ed.), *Travel and Tourism Encylopedia*. Travel World, 1959

Sampson, Anthony, *Empires of the Sky*. Hodder and Stoughton, 1984

Selby, Bettina, *Riding the Mountains Down*. Gollancz, 1984
—— *Riding to Jerusalem*. Sidgwick and Jackson, 1985

Seneca, *Letters from a Stoic*. Penguin Books, 1969

Shales, Melissa, (ed.), *The Traveller's Handbook*. Wexas, 1988

Cie G^{ie} TRANSATLANTIQUE *French Line*

LE "SOLEIL ROYAL"

LE "SOLEIL ROYAL"
Vaisseau de premier rang, construit en 1690.
Il était armé de 104 pièces de canon. Il prit part à
la bataille de la Hogue sous le commandement
de Tourville.
(D'après une aquarelle. – Bibliothèque Nationale)

MENU

Somerville-Large, Peter, *To The Navel of the World: Yaks and Unheroic Travels in Nepal and Tibet.* Sceptre, 1988

Stark, Freya, *The Southern Gates of Arabia.* Murray, 1936

—— *Dust in the Lion's Paw.* Murray, 1961

—— *The Journey's Echo.* Murray, 1963

Stevens, Thomas, *Around the World on a Bicycle.* London, 1887

Stevenson, Robert Louis, *Travels with a Donkey in the Cevennes.* London, 1879

Swinglehurst, Edmund, *The Romantic Journey.* Pica Editions, 1974

—— *Cook's Tours.* Blandford Press, 1982

Theroux, Paul, *The Great Railway Bazaar.* Hamish Hamilton, 1975

—— *Riding the Iron Rooster.* Hamish Hamilton, 1988

Thesiger, Wilfred, *Arabian Sands.* Longmans Green, 1959

Thubron, Colin, *Behind the Wall.* Heinemann, 1987

Turner, Louis and Ashe, John, *The Golden Hordes.* Constable, 1975

Twain, Mark, *Innocents Abroad.* Harper and Brothers, 1869

Vogue, *Travel in Vogue.* Macdonald, 1981

Woon, Basil, *The Frantic Atlantic.* Knopf, 1927

Young, Gavin, *Slow Boats to China.* Hutchinson, 1981

Young, Sir George, *Tourism, Blessing or Blight?* Penguin Books, 1973

Articles from the *Daily Telegraph, Departures, The Guardian, ITO World,* the *Journal of Travel Research, The Independent,* the *Observer,* the *Sunday Times, Time Out, The Times, Time Traveller, Tourism International History, Vogue, The Wall Street Journal* and other publications.

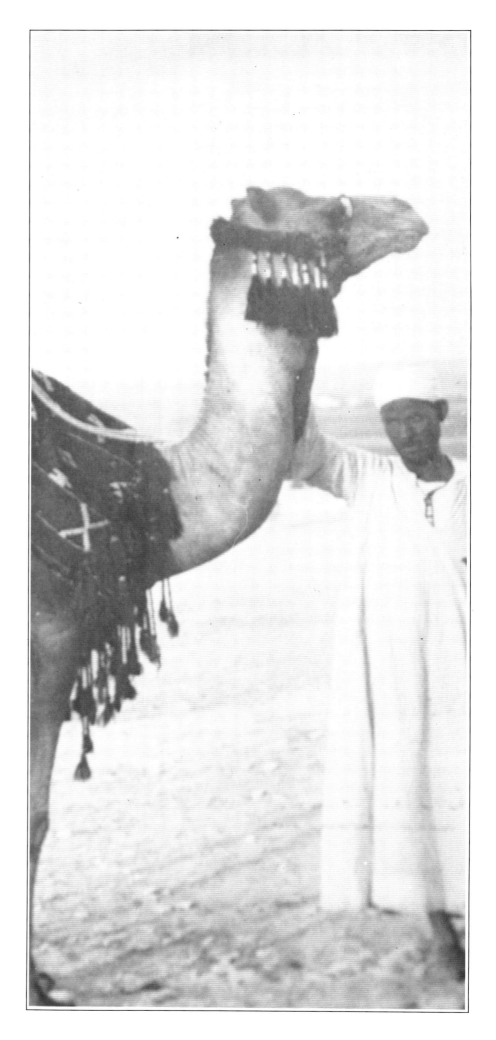

Picture Credits

c = centre, t = top, b = bottom, l = left, r = right

The publishers would like to thank the following
people and companies for their kind permission to
reproduce photographs:

American Express: 38, 115b, 118(2); John R. Clifford:
108–9, 130, 132–3, 139b; Peter Clifford: 7, 148t;
Mary Evans Picture Library: 13t, 47t, 113;
Gyldendal Norsk Forlag: 18(2); The Hulton Picture
Company: 1, 17, 21b, 22, 23(3), 26t, 28b, 29r, 32, 36,
50, 51, 54, 55, 58, 59(2), 69t, 69c, 70(2), 72t, 75(3),
76, 77b, 79, 80(2), 81, 84t, 89, 90t, 91(2), 92(2), 93t,
93b, 95, 96b, 99t, 100, 105(2), 120, 121b, 123, 124;
InterCity: 33, 125; Klick! International Photography:
126t; Adrian Meredith Photography: 83b, 96t, 107b;
Popperfoto: 20b, 63b, 73b, 82, 83t, 90b, 97, 99b, 129;
Dr R.J. Quinlan: 8–9; Royal Geographical Society:
11b, 12 (J. Holmes), 16 (C. Caldicott), 26b, 30, 44–5
(C. Caldicott), 62 (J. Holmes), 63t (J. Holmes), 74
(J. Holmes), 135c (C. Caldicott), 139c (S. Aarseth),
143b (S. Aarseth), 148b (Roger Mear); Travel
Images: 21t, 27t, 28t, 31, 56–7, 65(2), 84b, 110b,
143t, 145(2), 146–7, 149(2); Venice Simplon Orient
Express: 101(2), 102(3), 104(2); Viewfinder: 2, 10,
14–15, 19, 20t, 24–5, 291, 60, 61, 72b, 73c, 74b, 85,
86–7, 88, 107t, 110t, 112, 126b, 128, 131b, 135b,
136b, 138(2), 139t, 142, 144, 150(2), 151;

Any photograph not credited above has either come
from the Thomas Cook Archive or the publisher has
been unable to trace the source.

Acknowledgements

The author would like to thank the many
individuals and organizations whose specialist
knowledge and time were such an asset in the
preparation of this book, especially Edmund
Swinglehurst, the archivist of the Thomas Cook
Archive and his team Joy Hooper and Fiona Kelly,
and Fred Huntley and Ron Wilson of the British
Airways Archive. A very special thank you is owed
to Barbara Gilgallon whose research and help
were invaluable.